THE ARAB

THE HORSE OF THE FUTURE

BY

THE HON. SIR JAMES PENN BOUCAUT,
K.C.M.G.

SENIOR PUISNE JUDGE OF THE SUPREME COURT OF SOUTH AUSTRALIA
AND HERETOFORE THREE TIMES PRIME MINISTER
OF THAT STATE

PREFACE

BY

SIR WALTER GILBEY, BART.

AUTHOR OF

'RIDING AND DRIVING HORSES: THEIR BREEDING,' 'THE GREAT HORSE OR WAR HORSE,'
'HARNESS HORSES,' 'YOUNG RACEHORSES,' 'HORSES PAST AND PRESENT,' 'SMALL
HORSES IN WARFARE,' 'HORSE-BREEDING IN ENGLAND AND INDIA, AND ARMY
HORSES ABROAD,' 'HORSES FOR THE ARMY,' 'THOROUGHBRED AND OTHER
PONIES,' 'HUNTER SIRES'

1905

Copyright © 2013 Read Books Ltd.
This book is copyright and may not be
reproduced or copied in any way without
the express permission of the publisher in writing

British Library Cataloguing-in-Publication Data
A catalogue record for this book is available from the
British Library

Horses – Breeding and Anatomy

The horse (*Equus ferus caballus*) is one of two extant subspecies of *Equus ferus*. It is an odd-toed ungulate mammal belonging to the taxonomic family 'Equidae'. The horse has evolved over the past 45 to 55 million years from a small multi-toed creature into the large, single-toed animal of today. Humans began to domesticate horses around 4000 BC, and their domestication is believed to have been widespread by 3000 BC. We, as humans have interacted with horses in a multitude of ways throughout history – from sport competitions and non-competitive recreational pursuits, to working activities such as police work, agriculture, entertainment and therapy. Horses have also been used in warfare, from which a wide variety of riding and driving techniques developed, using many different styles of equipment and methods of control. With this range of uses in mind, there is an equally extensive, specialized vocabulary used to describe equine-related concepts, covering everything from anatomy to life stages, size, colours, markings, breeds, locomotion, and behaviour. Horse anatomy is a fascinating topic, and in the course of this introduction, the basics will be discussed.

To start; the horse skeleton averages 250 bones. A significant difference between the horse skeleton and that of a human is the lack of a collarbone—the horse's forelimbs are attached to the spinal column by a powerful set of muscles, tendons, and ligaments that attach the shoulder blade to the torso. The horse's legs and hooves are also unique structures. Their leg bones are proportioned differently from those of a human. For example, the body part that is called a horse's 'knee' is actually made up of the carpal bones that correspond to the human wrist. Similarly, the hock contains bones equivalent to those in the human ankle and heel. A horse also has no muscles in its legs below the knees and hocks, only skin, hair, bone, tendons, ligaments, cartilage, and the assorted specialized tissues that make up the hoof.

The hoof is one of the most important to study, and easily damaged parts of a horse. The critical importance of the feet and legs is summed up by the traditional adage, 'no foot, no horse.' The exterior hoof wall and horn of the sole is made of essentially the same material as a human fingernail. The end result is that a horse, weighing on average 500 kilograms (1,100 lb), travels on the same bones as would a human on tiptoe. For the protection of the hoof under certain conditions, some horses have horseshoes placed on their feet by a professional farrier. The hoof continually grows, and in most domesticated horses needs to be trimmed (and horseshoes reset, if used) every five to eight weeks, though the hooves of horses in the wild wear down and regrow at a rate suitable for their terrain.

One of the most important aspects of equine care is farriery. Farriers have largely replaced blacksmiths (after this specialism largely became redundant after the industrial revolution), and are highly skilled in both metalwork and horse anatomy. Historically, the jobs of farrier and blacksmith were practically synonymous, shown by the etymology of the word: farrier comes from Middle French *ferrier* (blacksmith), and from the Latin word *ferrum* (iron). Modern day farriers usually specialize in horseshoeing though, focusing their time and effort on the care of the horse's hoof, including trimming and balancing of the hoof, as well as the placing of the shoes. Additional tasks for the farrier include dealing with injured or diseased hooves and application of special shoes for racing, training or 'cosmetic' purposes. In countries such as the United Kingdom, it is illegal for people other than registered farriers to call themselves a farrier or to carry out any farriery work, the primary aim being 'to prevent and avoid suffering by and cruelty to horses arising from the shoeing of horses by unskilled persons.' This is not the case in all countries however, where horse protection is severely lacking.

The terrain horses originally inhabited is crucial to understanding their anatomy; horses are naturally grazing creatures. In an adult horse, there are 12 incisors at the front of the mouth, adapted to biting off the grass or other vegetation, with 24 teeth adapted for chewing. Stallions and geldings have four additional teeth just behind the incisors, a type of canine teeth called 'tushes.' Some horses, both male and female, will also develop one to four very small vestigial teeth in front of the molars, known as 'wolf' teeth, which are generally removed because they can interfere with the bit. As horses are herbivores, their grazing nature has resulted in a digestive system adapted to steady consumption of grasses. Therefore, compared to humans, they have a relatively small stomach but very long intestines to facilitate a steady flow of nutrients. Interestingly, horses are unable to vomit – so digestion problems can arise quickly, causing colic, a leading killer.

Horse breeds are loosely divided into three categories based on general temperament: spirited 'hot bloods' with speed and endurance; 'cold bloods', such as draft horses and some ponies, suitable for slow, heavy work; and 'warm bloods', developed from crosses between hot bloods and cold bloods, often focusing on creating breeds for specific riding purposes, particularly in Europe. There are more than 300 breeds of horse in the world today, developed for many different uses. The concept of purebred bloodstock and a controlled, written breed registry has become particularly significant; sometimes inaccurately described as 'thoroughbreds'. Thoroughbred is a specific breed of horse, while a 'purebred' is a horse (or any other animal) with a defined pedigree recognized by a breed registry. An early example of people who practiced selective horse breeding were the Bedouin, who had a reputation for careful practices, keeping extensive pedigrees of their Arabian horses and placing great value upon pure bloodlines. In the fourteenth century, Carthusian monks of southern Spain kept meticulous pedigrees of bloodstock lineages still found today in the Andalusian horse.

We hope the reader enjoys this book, and is encouraged to explore the world of horse breeding and anatomy for themselves.

'QUEEN VICTORIA'S FAVOURITE ARAB AND DOGS.'

From the painting by J. F. Herring senior, 1855, in the possession of Sir Walter Gilbey, Bart.

CONTENTS

CHAPTER		PAGE
	PREFACE BY SIR WALTER GILBEY, BART.	vii
I.	INTRODUCTORY	1
II.	DETERIORATION OF THE AUSTRALIAN HORSE	13
III.	DETERIORATION OF THE HORSE IN ENGLAND	26
IV.	CAUSE OF DETERIORATION	51
V.	THAT THE DETERIORATION HAS BEEN IN FALLING AWAY FROM THE ARAB	80
VI.	THE EXCELLENCE OF THE ARAB ACCORDING TO MAJOR-GENERAL TWEEDIE, GENERAL DAUMAS, AND THE GREAT EMIR ABD-EL-KADER	96
VII.	SUNDRY ENCOMIUMS ON THE ARAB TAKEN AT RANDOM, AND INSTANCES OF THE LOVE OF THE ARAB BY GREAT SOLDIERS	124
VIII.	HORSES OF ANCIENT ARABIA	176
IX.	MR. DAY AND THE DODO	195
X.	WHAT SORT OF HORSE TO BREED	204
XI.	WHAT OTHER COUNTRIES ARE BREEDING	224
XII.	CONCLUSION	239
	APPENDIX I	242
	APPENDIX II	244

LIST OF ILLUSTRATIONS

QUEEN VICTORIA'S FAVOURITE ARAB AND DOGS	*Frontispiece*	
		PAGE
THE AVERAGE HEIGHTS OF THOROUGHBREDS IN 1700, 1800, AND 1900		xiii
OWNER ON RAFYK	*To face*	32
QUAMBI STUD FARM, MOUNT BARKER SPRINGS, SOUTH AUSTRALIA	,,	64
SULEIMAN AND ZUBEIR	,,	96
RAFYK BEGGING FOR SUGAR	,,	128
MISS DE BEANGY (BY RAFYK OUT OF A HEAVY CART-MARE)	,,	160
SIR JAMES P. BOUCAUT ON FAROUN, BY MESSAOUD (SOLD TO RUSSIAN GOVERNMENT)	,,	192
RAFYK (ARAB STALLION)	,,	224

PREFACE

By SIR WALTER GILBEY, BART.

HAVING been requested by Sir James Boucaut to write a preface to the following chapters, I gladly consent, believing as I most firmly do that the Arab is the horse which has laid the foundation of all the best saddle-horses in England, America, India, and on the Continent.

Up to the present time more than 4,000 distinct works, in various languages, have been devoted to the horse, and among these are nearly ninety in Arabic and Persian, which are specially devoted to the Arab breed.

Careful research into the history of the horse shows that there have been two distinct types in England since Julius Cæsar visited our shores nearly 2,000 years ago—namely, the *light* horse and the *heavy* horse.

There can be no doubt whatever concerning the importance of the part which the Arab horse has played in the work of building up all our breeds of *light* horses.

The *heavy* horse* is a distinct type, and has been developed from the ancient British war-horse which evoked the admiration of Julius Cæsar. This breed of horse was the anxious care of Kings and Parliament from a date prior to the time of King John; and we find that the weight a riding-horse of this type had to bear, with its mail-clad rider and the plate-armour with which it was protected, might be upwards of 4 cwt., or 32 stone.

The writings of such authorities as Blundeville (1565), the Duke of Newcastle (1657), and others, give much information on the superior quality of the Arabian horses, and show that these animals were held in the highest esteem for breeding all saddle-horses.

Richard Berenger, the great authority on horses and horsemanship, in his book published in 1771, says: 'In taking a view of the horses most valued in the different part of the globe, *Arabia* stands most eminently distinguished for the excellence of its horses; and that it is from Arabian horses that the noblest breeds of Europe descend.'

Though the foundations of the English thoroughbred were laid only in the reign of King Charles II. by the importation of large numbers of stallions and mares, sires of Eastern blood had been brought to this country at frequent intervals from an early

---

* 'The Great Horse or the War Horse; from the Time of the Roman Invasion till its Development into the Shire Horse.' By Sir Walter Gilbey, Bart.; second edition, pubished 1899; Vinton and Co., 9, New Bridge Street, London.

period, and it is not difficult to understand why they were so prized by our ancestors.

Endurance and docility were the great essentials in the horses they sought to produce for hunting for ordinary use as saddle-horses, and as pack-horses to travel on narrow ways when roads did not exist in England. These essential qualities are still to be found in their highest perfection in horses of Eastern blood.

Until the time of King Charles II. (1660-1685), our racehorses (light horses) had not been graded into a distinct breed. This we learn from the writings of, among others, Richard Blome, whose work, 'The Gentleman's Recreation,' was published in 1686. Blome's advice to those who desired to breed racehorses, hunters, and road-horses is to choose a Turk, Barb, or Spaniard (all horses of Eastern blood) as the stallion, and to select the mare according to her shape and make, with an eye to the work for which the foal might be intended.

Our forefathers had no Stud-Book to guide them in their choice of stallion and mare; they were guided by their own judgment, and the pedigree of the stallion or mare could have weighed little or nothing with them—certainly nothing in the case of the sire, for they could have had no means of learning more of his pedigree beyond the fact that he was truly an Eastern horse.

The Byerly Turk, imported in 1689, was Captain Byerly's charger. He proved a most successful sire, and his stock (winners of many important races) are recorded in the early numbers of the General Stud-Book.

The Byerly Turk established the superiority of the Arabian stallions. He was used upon the Arab mares imported into England by King Charles, which have ever since been known as the *Royal Mares*, and the produce were found superior in speed on the turf and endurance to all other horses.

The importation of the *Royal Mares* furnished the starting-point for the grading up of modern racehorses.

The Darley Arabian, imported 1706, and the Godolphin Arabian, imported twenty-four years later, were exclusively used on the full-blooded Arab mares which were directly descended from the *Royal Mares* and the Byerly Turk who was imported in 1689.

Upton* proves beyond doubt, by his carefully compiled pedigrees, that the racehorses on the turf at the present time descend from these three sires and the *Royal Mares*.

The height of the Arabs originally imported into England averaged 14 hands, and our thoroughbred stock has been steadily graded up until the racehorses of late years—such as Macaroni, Parmesan, Caractacus, Ellington, Thormanby, etc., and those on the turf to-day—average $15 \cdot 2\frac{1}{2}$ hands.

* Roger D. Upton in his book 'Newmarket and Arabia,' published in 1873, by King and Co., London.

PREFACE   xiii

The following Plates illustrate the average heights of Thoroughbreds in 1700, 1800, *and* 1900.

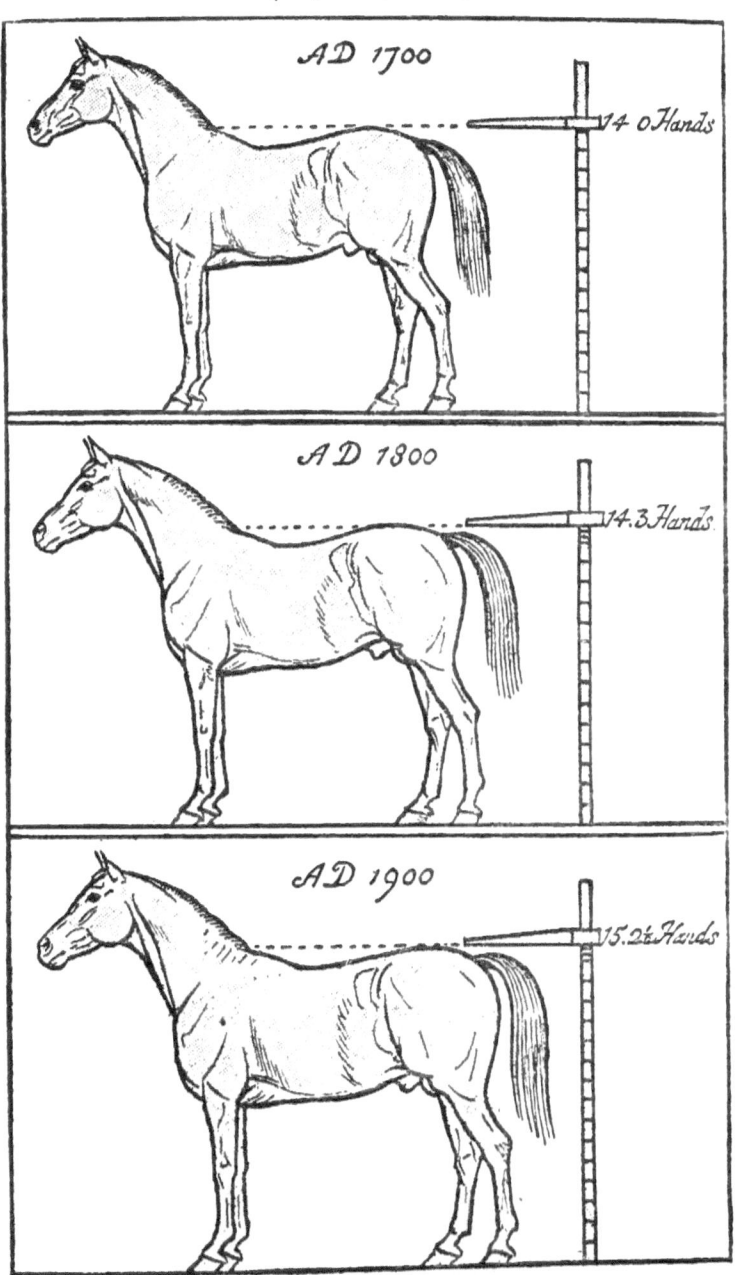

Since the old days of four-mile-heat races under heavy weights passed away, much has been sacrificed to speed over a short distance. The tendency for the past hundred years has been in the direction of shorter races and lighter weights; and breeders for the turf, regulating their policy accordingly, have succeeded in producing a longer-striding animal, which is much higher than his ancestors.

This increased height, and the greater speed it implies, has been obtained at the sacrifice of qualities less important to a successful turf career under modern conditions. This point is emphasized by Sir James Boucaut.

Admiral Rous, writing in the year 1860, said that the English racehorse had increased an inch in height in every twenty-five years since 1700.

As regards the desirability of reverting again to the Arab to improve our modern breeds of horses, whether in Australia or elsewhere, there can hardly be two opinions. The same forces have been at work in Australia as in England to produce deterioration in the thoroughbred: two-year-old races, short distances, and light weights leave all the best qualities of horse-flesh untaxed. They do more: they tend to develop delicacy of constitution.

Were the racehorse a breed entirely apart from all other breeds; were thoroughbreds used only and exclusively for the purpose of racing and of begetting racehorses; did they play no part whatever in the economy of horse-breeding apart from the turf, we might regard this deterioration with less concern; but, as everyone knows, the thoroughbred horse is used to 'improve' our hunters and saddle-horses.

Time was when the thoroughbred could do this: in the days when the racehorse ran four-mile heats under 11 or 12 stone, and ran such heats twice or three times on the same day; when, in a word, his Arab character had not been bred out of him to develop higher speed, he was admirably qualified to get hunters that would gallop and stay, saddle-horses that would carry weight, and troop-horses that could endure the hardships of campaigning on scanty fare. The misfortune is that the deserved reputation of the old-time thoroughbred has descended to the modern thoroughbred, which is a very different animal in size, make, shape, stamina, and constitution.

It is unreasonable to expect a horse which for a generation has been bred to gallop short distances at high speed to beget a horse that shall go all day under a heavy weight, at all paces, as the exigences of the chase may require. We have only to compare the make and shape of the typical modern racehorse with those of the heavy-weight hunter to see how impossible it is that he should do so.

To obtain improvement in all the best qualities of the horse—soundness, stamina, endurance, and docility—we cannot do better than revert to the pure Arab, which continues unspoiled by artificial treatment.

If it be objected that we shall lose height by using the Arab, the answer, furnished by experience in all parts of the world, is that height is the last consideration that need weigh with us in our endeavour to produce a useful type of horse. Mr. W. Scawen Blunt, whose experience in breeding Arabs, both in England and Egypt, is unequalled by that of any Englishman, made it his endeavour some years ago to increase the height of his pure Arab stock in Sussex.

Mr. Blunt found no difficulty in grading Arabs up a few inches, but having done so, he was forced to the conclusion that the merit of the horse does not increase in ratio with the height; and, recognising that the Arab averaging 14 hands 1 inch or thereabout was in all respects a more serviceable horse than the animal he had graded up 3 or 4 inches higher, he has since continued to breed Arabs to the height Nature determined for them.

Height is indispensable in the racehorse in order to obtain the necessary stride, but for real work the smaller and more compact horse has been proved infinitely superior. The small horse has greater staying-power, is not inferior as a weight-carrier, thrives on coarser food, and recovers sooner after exertion.

With scarcely an exception, the hackney sires of to-day descend in the direct line from the most beautiful of the three great 'foundation' sires—the Darley Arabian. The Darley Arabian begat Flying

Childers (the fastest racehorse of his day), Flying Childers begat Blaze, and Blaze begat the original Shales, from whom descended Danegelt and all the other typical hackneys whose names are to be found in the Hackney Society's Stud-Book.

It was through Blaze that Norfolk achieved fame more than a hundred years ago, for Blaze was the sire of Shales, foaled in 1755 out of a Norfolk mare. During the earlier years of the last century there still remained in the eastern counties of England the remnant of the trotting roadster stock for which Norfolk, as recorded by Mr. H. H. Dixon ('The Druid'), had 'almost European fame.'

The difference in make and shape between the thoroughbred and the hackney is due solely to the purpose to which either has been devoted for a long period of years.

None of the Continental Governments which devote attention to breeding horses pin their faith to one single type of horse, and depend upon that to establish all types. This statement applies particularly to France, Germany, and Hungary, where they have established distinct breeds for such purposes as artillery and cavalry work and harness.

They breed for business, not for pleasure; their aim is to produce the highest stamp of useful horse. With this definite object they have for sixty years and more been buying English mares, free from bias in favour of one strain or another. Geldinsg the foreign breeders scarcely ever purchase from

England. The large number of mares bought by them are those which have been accidentally blemished; but in all cases the shape, and not the pedigree, of the mare guides the purchaser. They also buy sound young mares for work, with the view of breeding from them afterwards.

In addition to their annual purchase of many thousand English mares, French and German breeders * have, since about 1830, been England's best customers for hackney stallions. They can now offer for sale from the great horse-rearing districts well-marked types of useful horses which they have gradually produced by judiciously mating the mares they have bought from England.

For this purpose the hackney was pre-eminently suited. Breeders of the hackney sought to perpetuate the qualities which made the ideal 'ride and drive' horse, and they have succeeded; for in the modern hackney we find the qualities which he has inherited from his sire, the Darley Arabian. Soundness, staying-power, docility, and handiness are characteristic of the well-bred hackney as they are of the Arab; and when the hackney has failed to maintain its reputation, it is because inferior sires have been selected and mated with unsuitable mares. The best sire cannot counteract all the defects of a bad mare in their joint produce.

* 'Horse-Breeding in England and India and Army Horses Abroad.' By Sir Walter Gilbey, Bart.; published 1901; Vinton and Co., London.

In no part of the British Empire is this question of building up a breed of horses suitable for saddle and harness work of more vital importance than it is in Australia. In that great colony, where stock-raising and sheep-farming are the foremost industries, where the distances to be traversed are great and roads are often indifferent, the saddle-horse fills the same place as it did in the mother-country until the 'golden age' of coaching.

The supply of horses that can travel at a fair pace all day and for days together has an interest for Australia which, unhappily for the interests of horse-breeding, is not felt in this country, with the network of railways covering its every corner.

With this ever-present need of such horses, Australia is fortunate in her possession of a climate and soil which are second to none in their suitability for horse-breeding. On the vast plains of the interior, horses enjoy all the advantages of a natural existence in a climate most favourable to their healthy growth, ranging, as they may, over great areas to pasture on the fresh and untainted grasses which, above all things, are necessary to the development and well-being of young stock.

The soundness of limb and freedom from chest and throat maladies enjoyed by Australian-bred horses is proverbial; and if two-year-old and short-distance racing has adversely affected the modern thoroughbred in the colony, her climatic advantages afford the opportunity of raising a fresh type which need not be subjected to the influences which have impaired the qualities of the old.

If the experiment upon which Sir James Boucaut is engaged can succeed anywhere, it will be in Australia, where all conditions are so favourable; and, having regard to the debt we owe the Arab horse in the past, it is to be earnestly hoped that the author's endeavour to open the eyes of his readers to the merits of the breed may induce others to follow his example, and help to restore in the horse of the future the characteristics of our horses of an earlier age.

ELSENHAM HALL, ESSEX,
1905.

THE ARAB THE HORSE OF THE FUTURE

CHAPTER I

INTRODUCTORY

I was led to attempt the formation of a stud of pure Arab horses in the State of South Australia principally by my love of the country, and a desire to be able to get away, at the end of the week, from the city and the books and chambers of the Supreme Court. After I had gotten me a place in the country, I was led into purchasing Arabs by finding that I required something when there to divert me, and as no one else had adopted that breed in our State, nor, as I believe, in Australia, and I believed that the pure Arabs would be eminently useful in renovating Australian horse-flesh, I started a little stud.

I had read so many accounts of the sad deterioration of Australian horses, especially of the thoroughbred, that I thought I should render a service to my adopted country by doing something that might improve the horse in Australia. I was the more induced to try Arabs because there is in the Australian interior very much of the same sort of dry country as is found on the borders of the Sahara and in Egypt and Arabia. I had learned, when stock-riding in the Bush in the forties, what a cross of the Arab blood was capable of. I thought that Arabs were more adapted for such a country than the larger, softer-bred English thoroughbred. As no one else, so far as I knew, had attempted breeding pure Arabs, I started the breeding—as I have said, principally as an amusement. Of course it has grown on me, as I suppose most hobbies do.

I had no mere sentiment about the matter. I joined with the racing gentlemen in laughing at the idea that the once fashionable song of the Arab steed was an authoritative exposition as to the Arab's excellence; all the same, it is founded, as was the adventure of Kenneth and Saladin in Sir Walter's Scott's 'Talisman,' upon the belief of forty centuries of men who knew—a belief which was well founded, which is again coming into vogue, and would never have been weakened but for the bookmaker and sprinting breeders. These have for some years past had the ear of a large section of the public in Australia, whose gambling propensities led them greedily to absorb the cult of the bookmakers, when there were very few found to say anything to the contrary, the encomiums on the Arab having been passed by as the froth of dreamers, or not noticed at all.

I do not propose to write a history of the Arab horse, nor even to attempt an original brochure on the subject; I have neither the special knowledge requisite nor leisure for the task. But I have had so many applications from all parts of Australia for information as to the stud of Arabs which I have started, and I find that there is so little known here about the breed, that I am desirous that the Australian horse-breeder (other than the racing-stud masters, some of whom know, perhaps, too much) should have an opportunity of learning something reliable about its quality, and therefore I have ventured to put together these observations on the subject. If we were to listen to some of the bookmakers and racing men, we should almost be led to suppose that the English thoroughbred is the only respectable horse in the world, and that the Arab horse does not exist at all, or, at least, that he only exists in romance, and was never a real living creature, and that his supposed good qualities were to be put down entirely to the dreams and fancies of some absurd poet or young lady songster.

It seems to me that the truth in this respect is that the most dangerous fancies with regard to the horse are the fancies of the racing gentlemen, who naturally look upon him as the implement of their occupation, whose love for him as a gambling machine has distorted history, and whose opinions on the subject are really misleading and erroneous. I do not blame them for this at all, but if some of these racing gentlemen could have been put upon their darling sprinters and turned out on the veldt to face the Boers in the late war, they would have altered their tune, as many sporting military officers, to their terrible discomfiture, were obliged to do.

In England, where there are large rival interests, and libraries and magazines, and of the making of books no end, the public has better opportunity for learning the Arab side—if I may use the term—of the question than we have here in Australia, where there are few libraries, not much making of books, and no large rival interests, so that practically only one side of the question has been prominently brought forward, or even heard of, except when occasional writers in a newspaper have thought it desirable to utter warnings.

Mr. Percy Rowland, in his recent book 'The New Nation,' comments on the lack of books in Australia, and the lack of respect for learning, which perhaps accounts for the lack of books.

Even in England the racing gambler and the bookmaker have had far too much influence in forming the opinion of the nation, as will be seen from what hereafter appears.

I propose in this little compilation to show, on the authority of some of the most experienced horsemen in the world, extending over long years—indeed, I may say long ages—that the sprinter is a huge mistake except for sprinting, and that the pure Arab of the desert is unequalled—also except for sprinting—in any station of life in which it 'may please God to call him.' I make no claim to original research, or to any knowledge whatever, on the subject of sprinting, except that which I get from the racing gentlemen themselves and from other well-informed persons.

It will, of course, be said that I am interested in the subject, as the owner of Arabs, and therefore that I am not a reliable authority. That is right enough. As I said, I am interested, and do not claim to be an authority. I form my opinion more upon what I have read than upon what I know. But I shall cite the statements of many, very many, of the most skilful horsemen and judges of horses who ever lived—their name, in fact, I may almost say is legion. I shall cite many, because the belief in the thoroughbred cult is so great and so widely spread, owing to the craze for gambling racing, that nothing but absolute demonstration often repeated will get rid of it in Australia. As a very great advocate, Lord Abinger, when at the Bar, replied in effect to one who asked him why he repeated himself so much in his speeches to the jury: 'You see, there are twelve fellows cram full of error, so that you have to repeat the truth again and again before you can knock it into all of them.' Also the *Times*, in December, 1903, explains the reason for its colossal advertising of the 'Encyclopædia Britannica': 'Because experience shows that the public require to be instructed over and over again before they can appreciate the slightest change from time-honoured methods.' I do not presume to instruct them; I only propose to give them some information which, I trust, may be useful.

I by no means desire to hold up the *Times* as equal in authority in all matters to the four Gospels, but I believe, on the whole, that it gives utterance to the concentrated common-sense of England. Therefore it is that I have felt justified in quoting its opinion on this, and the quotation just given is supported by another in the same paper, in the same spirit, in a leading article of March 11, 1904, on Army Reform. In justification of a statement made by Mr. Arnold-Forster in Parliament when exploding some utterly absurd charge, the *Times* says: 'The allegation is absurd to anyone who thinks, but there are so many people who do not think that there is hardly anything too absurd to require explicit refutation.' So on the subject that I am dealing with. Such a vast number of people never think at all, but adopt wholesale the most absurd assertions—as, for instance, that the English thoroughbred is a pure breed, and that the Arab is useless—that you may be excused for citing authorities to refute them. Indeed, as the *Times* puts it, you *must* do so: it is necessary to repeat again and again.

A country farmer who will pay no attention to the statements of two or three persons, may be led to think and inquire when he is referred to twenty or thirty, all practical men of the world, of great knowledge and experience, and to more than as many more travellers of all sorts and classes, who make similar assertions—especially when he finds that the opinion of the world, and of the greatest heroes and conquerors throughout all history, has been pretty much to the same effect, and that this opinion has generally prevailed, except during the comparatively recent development of gambling sprinting literature.

I am induced to be less sparing of citing authorities because a gentleman, who, I believe, is of considerable standing as regards his knowledge of horses, but whose name was not vouchsafed to me, stated a few weeks since to an intimate friend of mine in this State that it was all nonsense to praise up the Arab: he had neither speed, stamina, nor docility. This is in reality so utterly childish an assertion that it would not require serious refutation, were it not that the adoration of the English thoroughbred has been so intense, and has been indulged in of late by so many racing neophytes, that it seems really necessary, in common fairness, pretty fully to show that there is another side to the question.

I apologize to the reader if I have quoted too fully, but, as I have said, many quotations are necessary, and it would take half a lifetime properly to assort the material I should desire to lay before him; and at seventy-three time is not provided in very great excess of quantity.

The general consensus of opinion of an age is, of course, valuable, but, whether so or not, it is no good to breed the best for sale if most people think that the worst are better. People generally breed what they can sell. But certainly, before the opinion of an era can be of value, it ought to be founded on proper data and on consideration of both sides of a question.

Supposing, however, that I am unduly interested in favour of the Arab, that would not detract from the weight of the opinion of the many eminently neutral men whom I shall cite. The small amount of interest which I have on the one side is as nothing compared to the large amount of interest of the hundreds of breeders of thoroughbreds on the other side, who not only will not hear a single word in disparagement of their favourite, but will not hear a kind word said in favour of any other man's favourite, and ridicule any attempt in that direction. 'The thoroughbred' is English. Is that not enough? The placid contemptuousness of the Englishman for everything foreign comes in at once to satisfy him without inquiry that, as an Englishman is worth two Frenchmen any day, therefore no horse in the world can possibly equal an English horse!

Even if I do not get rid of my stock—I do not complain—I may lose a few hundreds, which I can set off against the pleasure I have had in breeding them; but if the breeders of thoroughbreds do not get rid of their surplus and useless stock, great numbers of persons lose heavily. Who are interested in supporting their side of the case? Not only the breeders themselves, but racing owners, trainers, grooms, jockeys, stable-boys, bookmakers, and sporting newspapers, not to mention vets, the makers of racing gear, and the runners of the 'tote.' All these from habit—they can't help it—are more or less constantly preaching sermons on the impeccability of the English thoroughbred. Indeed, there are at present but few men in Australia, largely interested in horses, whose interests are not more or less bound up with the thoroughbred breeders, for in this question breeders of heavy stock do not count. If the general public or the farming breeders should ever happen to think at all about the subject, they think as they have been educated from their youth up, having been taught to believe that the thoroughbred is the final outcome of everything that is wonderful in living matter. Beyond that they do not think, because most of them have no interest in thinking, and they have never heard anything to the contrary to make them think. It is therefore no wonder that very little has been heard about the Arab in Australia, the Arab thoroughbred—for thoroughbred he is, and he only: the wonder would be to have heard much.

It has often been said that 'the British public is a fool.' 'Thirty-nine millions, mostly fools!' I do not say it. I deny it. The saying is only a popular way of putting the advice of the *Times* in favour of much advertising. But when everybody tells the British public to fall down and worship the English thoroughbred, forthwith it does so—at least, it does so in Australia. Why not? Nobody says anything to the contrary. It does not much concern the public, so it has no call to think. Perhaps, however, some of my Australian fellow-colonists who are breeders of ordinary horses for useful purposes and who may read this little book, may deem it worth while to indulge in a thought or two. If they do, they will have plenty of material gathered in from many of the greatest men of the world.

I may for convenience' sake mention what I propose to show—viz. :

1. The general—indeed, almost universal—deterioration of thoroughbred horses both in England and Australia ; and if in England, necessarily in Australia, because most of the best sires here have come from England.

2. That the cause of the deterioration is chiefly the breeding for short-race gambling.

3. That the root of the English thoroughbred and all that is good in him is Arab.

4. The excellence of the Arab, and that he has not deteriorated.

5. That the most certain mode of recuperating the breed of saddle and buggy horses, and even of the thoroughbred himself, as a real racehorse, would

be the infusion of a large amount of pure and fresh Arab blood of the desert breed.

Notwithstanding the affected and adventitious worship of the English thoroughbred—it has almost become a religion—there is at bottom a nearly universal consensus of opinion as to his sad deterioration, and as to the cause of his deterioration. The opinion of one or two gentlemen might not be accepted, but on these points it is nearly everybody's opinion. The most sanguine and fanatic thoroughbred supporters hardly venture to affirm the contrary. I can find hardly a single man who does. They will tell you that the best horses are as good as ever, which I doubt. They may be as fast for short distances; the very statement that the best horses are as good as ever is pregnant with the admission that the general run is deteriorated, and that the breed, as a breed, is being ruined. And in the face of such opinions as I shall quote it would be foolish for the general horse-breeder to be further carried away by the 'thoroughbred cult' without making inquiry. The authorities I shall cite on this are irrefragable, and if there were any who pretended that the thoroughbred had not deteriorated before the Transvaal War, they have had to admit since that war that they were wrong. The Boers, mounted on their Arab ponies, laughed at the pick of our English and Australian horses, and literally ran rings around them. I have two sons who, with my consent, threw up their situations in my State to help the Empire, and joined Australian contingents to fight the Boers, so I claim to have something rather more than mere book-learning. *Vivâ voce* information giving the practical experience of practical soldiers who have fought hard is, I take it, somewhat more than book-learning.

Some of the writers of the Australian papers whom I quote may be occasional writers only, but many of them I understand to be regular contributors, and some of them on the regular staffs of the newspapers, and who therefore carry the authority of the papers with them. I may particularly refer to 'Bruni,' a writer on the *Australasian*, the leading weekly paper in Australia, who is a well-known and highly respected gentleman of the highest authority on horses and farm stock, and is so recognised throughout all Australia.

I wish most earnestly to say that I make no complaint of racing authorities; many I admire and respect. I make no complaint of gambling—I have nothing to do with that here; I only maintain that the gambling which has undoubtedly and notoriously sprung up around racing has led to a sad deterioration in the breed of English thoroughbred horses, and will lead to much greater deterioration if it be not checked.

CHAPTER II

DETERIORATION OF THE AUSTRALIAN HORSE

It is now well to notice the complaints to the effect that the Australian horse has greatly deteriorated.

These are universal, and have been rife for several years past throughout Australia. The old stock-horse of the forties and the fifties, which was celebrated for his staying powers, and could almost out-Arab Arabs, has departed. Most of these old stock-horses were largely imbued with Arab blood, imported into Sydney and Tasmania from Bombay, before the time of steamers, and when the voyage from England was such a terror.

I can speak to a certain extent as to this from personal knowledge. I was a stock-keeper from 1847 to 1850, and I assert unhesitatingly that you cannot nowadays 'get the likes' of the old overland stock-horse, either for love or money. They had nothing but the native grass, and 'could go for ever.' On one occasion in 1847, at Kingsford, six miles beyond Gawler, just as dinner was being laid—the dinner-hour was at one—the late Mr. Stephen King, a well-known stock-owner, afterwards Special Magistrate, sent me to Adelaide, thirty-two miles off, to get to the bank before three, and started me without dinner, because the matter was of importance. I got into the bank at Adelaide comfortably before three, and got home again comfortably before dark. I rode my stock-horse fresh off the run—there were no paddocks then—and with a good feed the old horse could have repeated the journey before morning This fine old beast was half Arab from Tasmania. I loved him almost as well as any human being, except my own family—better, indeed, than I loved some people.

It is strange, but it seems to me that the Arab and the half-bred Arab, where he takes after the Arab ancestor, has a singular capacity for winning the affection of his rider. Dr. Wills, in his 'Modern Persia,' says that Periam, in telling the story of his horse being killed, left off 'with wet eyes.'

Mr. C. B. Fisher, a very old colonist of this State and a grand old English gentleman, universally respected beyond most men in Australia, importer of Fisherman, and one of the best breeders, importers, racers, and amateur riders of racehorses, who ever lived in Australia (after whom the C. B. Fisher race is named), says 'unhesitatingly' (*South Australian Register*, September 18, 1902) that you don't get horses to go now seventy, eighty, or ninety miles straight out of the paddock as you used; that he once took a horse out of the paddock with his belly full of grass, and rode him sixty-four miles in eight hours. Horses had better stamina then. Mr. Fisher's opinion is of the greatest weight on this point, as he has been all his life more or less connected with racehorses, breeding and racing racehorses, and his natural prejudice would therefore seem to be in favour of the thoroughbred and his present breeding.

My father in the early fifties, living at Sarnia, five to six miles south of Adelaide, used frequently to visit my sister living at Manoora, seventy-five miles north of Adelaide, always doing the journey each way in one day—eighty miles—and thought nothing special of it. As Mr. Fisher says, you don't get horses to do that now.

Mr. J. M. Borrow, a very old colonist of this State, hearing that I was contemplating an article on the subject, writes me to the same effect as Mr. Fisher's statement, and says that Mr. H. S. Price, a former owner of Canowie, used often to ride a horse which he had, with Arab blood in him, from Canowie to Adelaide, a distance of 130 miles, within the twenty-four hours, and offers to furnish other instances of similar staying-power of the old semi-Arab stockhorse.

In the sixties I rode a pony, half Arab, half Timor, belonging to my sister, from Netley to Ketchowla, eighty miles. I went through the Bush, there being no track, which made the distance greater, between 8 a.m. and 11 p.m. The gallant little beast could have gone on for half as far again with comfort.

As it was, I should have got in some considerable time before eleven, only I had to go out of the way to a friendly station to borrow a remount for my brother, who was with me and whose own horse had knocked up. Dr. J. P. Ryan, of Melbourne, told me, that, in August, 1894, the late Mr. Henry Ricketson, a large stock-holder, owner of several stations, some years ago rode a horse, whose sire was an Arab, over 100 miles within the twenty-four hours. He started at half-past two in the morning, to overtake a drover with cattle, and came up to him by nine the same evening.

Mr. Walter Hickinbotham, a great Australian trainer, recently stated, in a reported interview in Adelaide, that the provincial horses in old days were a lot better stayers and of finer qualities than can be met with in the country towns now; and he asks how many horses could do to-day what Swiveller, which he bred in 1874, did; Swiveller travelled 800 miles, then won three races and ran three seconds. And when pointedly asked if he thought the horses of to-day were as good as they were in the sixties and seventies, replied that they were not so stout, and were not such good stayers, but were faster. Of course they are faster for short distances—they are bred for that, no matter what other quality is lost; but for the veldt, or the road, or the Bush, a good stout stager, not a sprinter, is wanted.

In some reminiscences of racing (*Express*, May 28, 1904) it is affirmed that they would be incomplete if they did not recall the difference between the old times and now: that it required more than speedy weeds to win the events of those days. The inference is, of course, plain, that now the winners are merely speedy weeds.

The *Leader*, a great Victorian weekly (October 6, 1890), points out that the Auckland Association, a New Zealand Society, submitted to the Minister two chief causes for the preponderance of unsuitable animals, one cause being unfit stallions; and a letter-writer in that same paper verifies the statement that there is a lamentable want of good stallions; yet the New Zealand horses are said to be better than the Australian horses. The stallions are unfit because their best qualities have been bred out of them in favour of sprinting.

'Carbine,' writing in the *Queenslander*, the great country paper of Queensland (April 25, 1891), where large numbers of horses are bred, says that it is admitted on all sides that of late years stayers have been exceedingly scarce in England, putting short-distance races as the cause, and stating that in Australia we are following the bad example. But even without breeding for short-distance racing here, it would follow that if we get all our best blood from England, and that is bad, we can expect nothing else but bad here. If the best blood which Australia can get from England cannot stay, and if Australia breed from that, so as to be able to sprint, how can Australia expect to get her horse-flesh to stay?

'Ghora Wallah,' writing in the *Australasian* (December 11, 1898), quotes an Indian paper as describing Australian horses at the time as 'useless brutes—ill-bred, nervous, ugly, soft-hearted, and sickly brutes.' That is not much to be proud of. He then affirms that the demand for Australian horses in India was owing to the fact that it is now next to impossible to secure a good Arab. This quotation is what may be termed ' a double banker.' It proves, first, that the Australian was in his opinion 'a sickly, useless, ill-bred brute,' and, secondly, that great confidence is placed in India in the Arab. The uselessness and ugliness of the Australian may perhaps here be somewhat exaggerated; I thoroughly believe that it is. But if Australia seeks to sell horses, it must meet the views of its customers, and, from ' Ghora Wallah's ' remarks, it is evident that if India could get pure Arabs in sufficient number, she would not take Australian horses at all. That should be a strong incentive to Australians to breed Arabs or from Arabs. The accuracy of ' Ghora Wallah's ' statement on this will receive abundant verification hereafter.

A. B. Patterson, in the *Sydney Mail*, confessed that our Australian horses in the Transvaal War were not as good as many sent by other countries, and said that it was a fact that there were no good remounts to be got in Australia now in large numbers, no matter what price was paid.

'Bruni,' to whom I have referred, wrote in the

Australasian (October 26, 1901) that never before were there so many complaints of want of constitution, bone, endurance, and ability to carry weight, made against the thoroughbred as at the present time. And in another article he said that our general run of horses is not nearly so good as it was many years ago. On April 11, 1903, he wrote that the best lovers of the turf in England had bewailed the strong tendency to deterioration that had been manifested in the English racehorse during the last quarter of a century, and that that was the result of breeding for speed. He quoted a modern writer on the annual sale of thoroughbred yearlings at Doncaster a few years ago, who said that it was anything but flattering to see so many with bad forelegs—'quite stilts, in fact.' Then he applied the lesson to Australia, and showed that it was not a few horses, no matter how brilliant their performances, that made up a breed, but that it was the standard of excellence of the majority that constituted the value of the race, and said that it was a great misfortune that the breeders of thoroughbred horses had come to regard their *raison d'être* as purely for racing purposes. Then he asked how long would one of those spindle-shanked weeds that he saw daily going to the Flemington training-ground last in a forty minutes' run with the Pytchley, and affirmed that if they got into a ploughed field they would not be likely to get out of it. Flemington is the Garden of Eden of horse-flesh, where the Melbourne Cup is raced for. As Bruni's argument shows, it is of little use to have one Carbine, or even ten Carbines, if you breed from a hundred sickly weeds.

The *Daily Telegraph* (Sydney, June 16, 1900) said that the veriest weeds frequently win prizes — horses that would drop before a few miles were covered; that there was urgent need for improvement in bone, stamina, and weight-carrying character; and that the Australian horse was gradually deteriorating in bone and sinew, and therefore in staying power. How absolutely true were these remarks the Transvaal War bitterly taught us.

The *Australian Pastoralists' Review* (November 5, 1900) affirms that again we are face to face with the most deplorable deterioration of the horse of the British Empire.

The Australian Press telegrams from London, March 4, 1902, state that Lord Kitchener had complained that the Australian horses were especially badly selected, and that Colonel Birkbeck, Inspector of Remounts at Cape Town, reported that the New South Wales horses were sadly disappointing, and that the draught-horses were 'a positive scandal.' Considering that great pains had been taken in Australia to select these horses, and that great credit had been given to many of the selectors, it says but little for the Australian horses which are left in the Commonwealth, when those so carefully selected are pronounced by Lord

DETERIORATION OF THE AUSTRALIAN HORSE

Kitchener to be especially badly selected, and by Colonel Birkbeck to be sadly disappointing. Three hundred and nine thousand horses had been supplied to the troops in South Africa up to the end of January, 1902, of which only 20,000 had been supplied from Australia. Is it not lamentable that such a small number of our picked cattle should have called forth such condemnation from Lord Kitchener and Colonel Birkbeck?

A Minister in the House of Commons (March 17, 1902) said that the Government had taken an enormous number of horses from Australia, but that it was difficult to get those small compact horses that the Government required. I pray breeders to take note of this song, sung again and again—'Wanted, small compact horses.'

The owners of one of the best-known stations on the Dawson wrote of some of the horses bred in Queensland, that they were rubbish, a disgrace to the men who bred them, and that they must know that their horses were going back. Of course they knew it. But there have been two difficulties in the way of getting better: first, vested interests and the pæans of racing breeders, who from habit and education laud their racers; and, secondly, the difficulty—almost impossibility—of getting better.

These two things have led them to breed from creatures 'which ought never to have appeared in the Stud-Book.'

The *South Australian Register*, a leading Adelaide daily (August 18, 1902), says that the deliberate opinion of an officer of the 11th Hussars, expressed some months ago, was that never before had such a collection of inferior horses been gathered together. His opinion was supported with marked emphasis by Lieutenant Sydney Galvayne in his book on 'War-Horses, Present and Future; or, Remount Life in South Africa,' who called the Australian drafts 'a most wretched lot.'

The Australian Stud-Book, vol. vi., has a list of Colonial-bred stallions, in respect of which it observes: 'Many stallions under this heading are not worthy of entry, but as they have been bred from they are included.' This observation is entitled to special weight, considering where it appears, and considering that it is, as it were, a sidelight amounting to an unintended testimony of deterioration. The writer did not want to 'quarrel with his bread-and-butter,' so did not give names. That he made the statement at all in such a book is proof that he is a conscientious gentleman. I do not complain that he did not give names; but one scabby sheep infects the whole flock, and fifty clean rams cannot get rid of it. Who can say to what extent these creatures 'not worthy of entry' have poisoned the horse-blood in Australia? There is prepotent influence in heredity, but to be useful it must be wisely directed. Mr. Robert Bruce, of the Irish Agricultural Department, warns breeders that pedigree ill applied is harmful and dangerous. He says 'it is well for breeders to recognise that defects in form and constitution intensify at an alarming rate.'

Dr. Chapple, writing recently on 'The Fertility of the Unfit,' says that all these defectives are prolific, and transmit their fatal taints. The proportion of habitual criminals is steadily on the increase, and was never so high as now. It seems the same in racing horse-flesh.

W. H. Lang wrote in the *Australasian* (June 28, 1902) that we were not improving the breed of horses, and were in a much worse position as regards our saddle and harness horses than before; and he adds the most suggestive observation, that he has met no one who says that we have improved, and he does not think that Diogenes with his lantern could find anyone who does think so.

'Faneargh,' in the *Mount Barker Courier*, a weekly paper published near Adelaide, appealing to a large country district (May 2, 1902), wrote that it is a difficult matter to obtain a young, sound, well-broken horse free from vice and yet of decent appearance.

Major-General Viscount Downe, C.B., spoke of Australian horses (*vide* telegram in the Adelaide papers, October 21, 1902) as being mere weeds, lacking in the substance necessary for a cavalry charger.

Major-General Plumer told the Royal Commission on the War that the little horse will do with less food than the big Australian horse; that the latter starves on a ration that the South African pony thrives on. I venture to say that it is not a mere question of ration; if that were so, the remedy would be easy—give him another ration. But it is a question of breed. The big Australian horse is soft, the little one nearly pure; consequently, in difficulties the one was all funk, the other full of pluck to the end. The little one was, I take it, Arab. Major-General Plumer's criticism was as to the big horse as contrasted with the little one.

A writer (I have the print, but have lost the name and date), quoting the *Live Stock Journal* and 'Impecuniosus,' says that for many years past the English thoroughbred has been bred for speed alone, and that the great qualities of strength, stoutness, and courage, for which the breed was once famous, have been completely ignored. He asks, 'What cross-bred horse could be as well fitted to produce hunters as old Panic?' And he says that there were fifty years ago any number of equally stout thoroughbreds, but that at the present day they are few and far between. In their absence he affirms that no better sire than such a sound Arab as that mentioned by 'Impecuniosus' could be wished for as a sire for hunters.

Lord Kitchener wired to the Queensland Government that the *Victoria* might 'be fitted up with as many small stout horses as she can carry'; and his lordship in a telegram (December 11, 1900) says: 'English horses arriving are still too heavy; a well-bred weight-carrying polo pony is the ideal required for all mounted troops who carry little on the saddle.' This shows that Lord Kitchener was alive to the evil of the 'five or six crosses of thoroughbred' pampered up into bigness.

The London *Times* says that Lord Downe's report gives damnatory evidence to show that there was a larger proportion of horses of an entirely unsuitable class, in some cases amounting to 50 per cent., and affirms that the Cape Colony and Basuto pony was the best horse, and from 14 to 15 hands the best size.

I have no doubt that many scores of other authorities to the same effect could be produced, but I have not searched for any. I have only put together those which have incidentally come under my notice in general reading.

CHAPTER III

DETERIORATION OF THE HORSE IN ENGLAND

IT will appear plainly, from what has been written above, how greatly horses have deteriorated of late in Australia. Some of the authorities cited have shown that they must have deteriorated in England also. But this chapter will give some particulars of how greatly they have thus deteriorated.

Sir Walter Gilbey, Bart., in a recent book,* points out that seventeen years ago he drew attention to the deterioration of the horse in England, and asks if our position to-day is any better than it was in the year 1884, and then proceeds to show that it is worse. Not merely as bad, but worse. He quotes Colonel Hallen as saying that, while the animal got by the English thoroughbred is as a rule handsome, he is often shallow in girth and back rib, light in barrel, and from 70 to 80 per cent. of them are leggy and deficient in bone and limb. He points out that diseases of the legs are more common among thoroughbred stock—*e.g.*, curb, bone-spavin,

---

* 'Horse - Breeding in England and India, and Army Horses Abroad.'

bog-spavin, and ringbone, which are not infrequently shown; that few of this stock prove fit for the British cavalry, and hardly one for the horse or field artillery. What Colonel Hallen said was written in 1888, and how true it was the Boer War has demonstrated.

Mr. Fred Adye, in his book on horse-breeding (1903), says that there is perhaps a popular impression that the British cavalry horse is the best horse in the world, but that the impression, if it exists, is a very erroneous one. The physique both of men and horses at recent military manœuvres in Wilts and Dorset had greatly deteriorated since 1872. Squadron after squadron passed by, and 'not a good horse could we discover among them. There was uniformity of bad points. All seemed to be both light and coarse, plain heads, upright shoulders, no back ribs to speak of, and drooping quarters.' And he adds that the opinion of Indian cavalry officers was that the Indian cavalry, at any rate in a long campaign, would ride round the British; that their horses, though smaller, being so much better shaped and bred, it was the opinion of many experienced officers that, could Indian cavalry* have been used in Africa, the war would not have lasted half as long as it did. He said the general supply of horses has not of late years been equal either in quality or quantity to what it formerly was. What can we think of our boasted English cavalry?

Sir Walter Gilbey was not content with his book,

* Largely Arab.

but wrote a letter to the *Times* so lately as March 12, 1902, in which he said that horse-breeding was going from bad to worse in England. Of course it would be so, because the same causes were operating from day to day in almost geometrical ratio, and the influence of racing men was so great that people would not trouble to think till the Boer successes brought it home to their minds with such terrible results.

Breeders in Australia, and, I believe, also breeders in England, are beginning to realize—and they will not improve their horse-flesh until they do thoroughly realize—the fact that to breed for horse-racing is not to breed for use, and that the worst of sires is a weedy thoroughbred. It may be that at one time racing improved the breed of horses, although even that is doubtful. It does so no longer, and to affirm that it does is a sham—one of those huge shams for which these latter days are so notorious.

So long ago as 1874, Mr. De Vere Hunt, in his book 'England's Horses in Peace and War,' wrote that England stood in great danger of really losing the horse altogether as a sound and useful animal because of the many causes that had been for many years progressively co-operating to deteriorate. He might now almost ask, 'Have we not lost him? Is he not bred out?'

He wrote of Ireland that the deterioration of the breed of horses must be considered as an evident and acknowledged fact, and amongst the causes he placed the carelessness with regard to brood mares and stallions, the dearth of good stallions, and the consequent improbability that the poor horse-breeders could make use of a superior but expensive sire, and the introduction generally of fashionable rather than sound and useful blood. 'Fashionable blood!' Hyde Park! And he adds to these causes the purchase of our best horses for foreign Governments, whose agents were ever on the look-out for our best horses, over the sale of which we had no control. Plain common-sense men will do well to note the word 'fashionable,' which means, of course, what the fad of the day approves of. The fad of the day is sprinting and tall, leggy animals for the parks. Rudyard Kipling's 'flannelled fools' of the wicket, Captain Upton's 'dandies,' make the 'fashion,' partly by the influence of the bookmaker and the trainer, and partly because they think they show off better on such creatures. Is it not time that the farmer, the breeder for use, the War Office, and the gentlemen of England, set their faces against such a fashion?

Mr. Sydney Galvayne, in his 'War-Horses, Present and Future,' speaks of the English horse as 'a pampered stock,' 'not the animal he is supposed to be,' 'not in it for saddle purposes,' 'not having one single recommendation'; and, as before mentioned, of the Australian drafts to South Africa—of course, descended from English horses—'as a most wretched lot.'

Mr. William Day, in his book on the horse (1900), commenting on the Hunter and Stallion Classes at the Show of the Royal Agricultural Society of England at Newcastle, quotes a reviewer as saying that of one of the best collections of thoroughbred stallions ever seen, to judge them by appearances, out of thirty-six stallions exhibited, twenty-four were disliked—ten for having bad feet or legs or defective hocks, two for unsoundness, two more as hopelessly suffering from the same affliction. On which Mr. Day observes that out of thirty-six picked stallions, supposed to be the best of the sort in England, no less than fourteen (perhaps more if all had been examined) were considered by the judges not fit for the purpose. So bad, indeed, had things got to be that Mr. Day states that a well-known dealer had discontinued his visits to the West, where formerly he used to procure most of his horses, as there were none then to be had.

An article in the *Rapid Review*, September, 1904, says that it is calculated that 1,400 two-year-olds make their début on a racecourse every season, but only a dozen or so remain good enough to go to the post for the Derby—perhaps 1 per cent. Out of how many thousands the 1,400 are picked I have no means in Australia of discovering.

Mr. Day also says that unsoundness does exist inherent in all horses to a great extent, and though the cause may be obscure the fact is patent. Upon which I observe that the cause is not obscure. It is because the creature has been bred only as an article to gamble with, and his useful qualities ignored. He quotes 'Stonehenge' as affirming that one chief difficulty of the trainer now is to keep his horse sound, and that, unfortunately, as disease was in most cases hereditary, and too many unsound stallions were bred from, the difficulty is yearly on the increase; and then he refers to 'roaring' and 'enlarged joints' as being 'the rule instead of the exception.'

In another place he says that, in spite of the best food and the sparing of no expense or labour, there was no class of horses among which the mortality was so high as it is among our thoroughbred stallions, and the appalling proofs of this could be cited in abundance. Note the word 'appalling.' This from Mr. William Day, the great racing authority! Why, if you could make a hybrid between a racehorse and a cow, things could not be very much worse than is depicted by Mr. William Day, probably the greatest racing trainer we ever had in England, and who is often cited as proving the excellence of the English thoroughbred.

In another book, 'The Racehorse in Training,' Mr. Day says that year after year trainers have sent to them large, heavy-shouldered, slack-loined, little-legged brutes that would fall over a straw. He advises breeders to breed sound animals, instead of breeding, as most do, from any crooked-legged, deformed brutes, if only they have a brother's or sister's fame to recommend them, and he vouches that he has seen yearlings sold for 1,000 to 1,500 guineas apiece, or double, which were not worth sixpence for the purpose for which they were bought. Not worth sixpence!

He expresses his sympathy for the purchaser of one of these sensational flat-catchers, which had been disposed of to some unfortunate individual, and ingenuously relates how by a 'stratagem'—note the admirable word!—he helped some such unfortunate individual who was a friend to get rid of such a useless creature by palming him off on some other unfortunate individual who, I suppose, was not a friend. Mr. Day naïvely writes, 'we succeeded beyond our expectation.' Doubtless 'Wapstraw,' possessing this useless creature, caused his hopeful offspring to go about in gaiters, with riding-breeches, open-mouthed, boasting that their weedy purchase was 'a thousand-pounder, sir!' And the youths of the district gape and admire, and the fathers send their mares to visit him.

In an article on 'Thoroughbreds in 1897' in the *Live Stock Journal* Almanack for 1898, by C. B. Pitman, it is stated that Persimmon was so shaken by his race on the hard ground at Sandown that it was not deemed prudent to let him fulfil his autumn engagements at Newmarket, and yet it is stated of this same Persimmon and of St. Frusquin that in them 'we had two colts of rare excellence.' Further on Mr. Pitman states that in the sale of thorough-

OWNER ON RAFYK SADDLED.

breds for 1897 the four-figured yearlings were only twenty-four in number, and fetched 25,950 guineas, whereas in 1896 thirty-two yielded 51,250 guineas, and he regretfully adds that the almost unbroken failure of these expensive colts and fillies is evidently making itself felt. Persimmon! the great horse of His Most Gracious Majesty the King! This is trumpet-tongued, not only because of the means of knowledge and the sources of information at the command of His Majesty, but because we may be perfectly sure that his popularity and the loyalty and admiration felt for him would make everyone in any way concerned with his horses extremely anxious to do the very utmost that could possibly be done to give him satisfaction and to avoid allowing him to become possessed of an inferior animal. And Mr. Charles Richardson says in his book on the Turf that Persimmon was fairly entitled to be called the best horse of his year!

If this is found to be the case with the very pick of the picked stock of England ('the £1,000 yearlings'), what is to be thought of the ruck? Sir George Chetwynd, in his racing reminiscences, says that there are hundreds of five-furlong and six-furlong sprinters, but the real stayers you could almost count on your fingers, and that even then it was a pitiable sight to see the way some of the men are mounted in our first-class cavalry regiments. This was years before the Boer War. Again I ask, Is it a wonder that the Boers laughed at us? Is it not a crime to entrust the lives of our soldiers, and it may be the honour and existence of the nation, to such pampered 'weeds'? Mr. William Day supports Sir George Chetwynd in speaking as to the best judges giving high prices for useless animals.

Blackwood's Magazine, in an article in June, 1900, on 'English Cavalry,' says that it was tolerably well known that in South Africa, at any rate, our English troop-horses had altogether collapsed, and had exhibited a lack of stamina as certain as it was deplorable; that when they were called upon for prolonged effort under the uncertain conditions of real war, they had no reserve of constitutional endurance and vigour on which they could fall back. The writer added that many people thought—and apparently with much reason—that in our country the standard was really depreciating. Many people 'thought'! Why, most people 'knew.'

What man of common-sense, after reading all this, can upon the question of breeding accept as final the judgment of those who have brought about the state of collapse above depicted? Is it not time to stop, and to begin *de novo*?

C. B. Pitman (*Live Stock Journal* Almanack, 1902), five years after his former comment, says that the story of the thoroughbred in 1901 was one of continued failures and disappointments, and it could not be said that there was a redeeming feature—the trail of mediocrity was over them all; that for a short time after the St. Leger it was possible to cherish the delusion that the three-year-olds were not as bad; that it was no better when we came to the two-year-olds, where the disappointment was all the greater because so much was expected.

Captain Upton quotes an article some few years ago in the *Times* which says that the qualities of the English racehorse were certainly on the decrease, and aged running horses and mares had disappeared from our racecourses, although yearlings offered under the hammer were on the average growing larger and stronger; but he points out that the appearance of strength is fallacious, and that bigness is no criterion—a view now abundantly demonstrated.

Mr. Joe Thompson, known throughout Australia as a leading bookmaker, universally respected, who has lately practised in England, wrote towards the end of 1903 that there were then very few long-distance horses in England, and he thought the Frenchmen could beat the English easy; but that that year at Ascot for the greatest long-distance weight-for-age race the English were represented by not even good handicappers. The consequence was that the Frenchmen, *with only ordinary horses*, won easily.

I don't suppose that in all Australia there is any man whose word would be taken before Mr. Thompson's, and his assertion that the Frenchmen, with only ordinary horses, won easily is very startling evidence as to English inferiority.

Even 'Cecil,' who published a rather famous book on the stud-farm, and is decidedly a friend of the thoroughbred, and who maintains, on the whole, the non-degeneration theory, says (1873) that in every district 'the most unsound, weedy wretches go the circuit,' and that roaring is an infirmity that has increased of late years amongst thoroughbred horses rather extensively; that there were not so many inferior horses brought to the post of yore as when he wrote; that handicaps did not before then induce to the cultivation and training of useless weeds; and he shows how severe training and racing impair constitutions, and have a most injurious influence over some animals, which in many instances they never overcome. All this, and more, from an advocate for non-degeneration! And matters have become worse since.

Major Arthur Griffiths, late of the 63rd Regiment, in his book on the English army (1878), says that there is an increasing scarcity of the proper kind of horses required to meet the current demand. The question of their supply is yearly growing into more serious proportions, and he criticises the decision of a Committee of the House of Lords not to employ Government stallions, although it was not denied that the produce was already deteriorating from the inferior quality of the entire horses which travelled the country. Then comes his reflection that to adhere too rigorously to the views he combats 'is to sleep on in a fools' paradise from which some day there may be a rude awakening.' Colenso! Stormberg! Magersfontein! Were they not a rude awakening? He regrets that the advice of Captain Nolan, of Balaclava fame, was 'for the most part unheeded, and cavalry regiments lapsed more and more into the hands of the dandies and the barrack square martinets . . . fine gentlemen who never identified themselves with their men.' These, I suppose, are the gentlemen who had the selection of the horses for Omdurman, which had to be left behind at Cairo, some of them probably the 'dandies' of Captain Upton.

Mr. G. W. Steevens, in his book 'With Kitchener to Khartoum,' in describing the start of the British Egyptian army at five in the morning to ride forth to Omdurman, says that at the first glance the British cavalry looked less like horsemen than like Christmas-trees. What made the likeness to Christmas-trees was the fearful loads they were carrying, and which he enumerates: 'picketing pegs lashed to carbines, feeds of corn hanging from saddles, canvas buckets opposite them, waterproofs behind bulky holsters, in front bundles of this thing and that dangling here and there, water-bottles in nets under the horses' bellies, khaki neck-screens flapping from helmets'; and then he continues: 'The smallest Syrian—they had left their own big hungry chargers in Cairo—had to carry 18 stone; with a heavy man the weight was well over 20.' That is not quite so much as was carried by the Barbs of the French cavalry in Africa, mentioned by General Daumas; but the 'big hungry chargers'—*i.e.*, the English horses—couldn't carry the load nor do the work, so they had to be left behind.

The Syrian horses are certainly Eastern horses, and have been described as Arabs—inferior Arabs. Could there be found a more damning reference to the deterioration of the English horses than this? So utterly useless were they in the field that the 'big hungry' brutes had perforce to be left behind in Cairo? Could there be more eloquent testimony in favour of the Arab than this, that the little Syrian Arab had to be called in to do the work that the English horse was incompetent to do? Then Mr. Steevens gives the lesson which he derived from the incident, which he says was a better lecture in cavalry than many text-books. Part of the lesson was that it is not the weapons that make the cavalry-man, but the mobility; not the lance he charges with, but the horse that carries him. The lesson, alas! was lost upon the gentlemen who played polo at Ladysmith, the 'dandies' of Major Arthur Griffiths; so the Boers for two years laughed us to scorn.

The *Windsor Magazine*, January, 1903, has it that the enemy was always getting away when he ought to have been caught, because our horses were unequal to the work required of them. Many a victory was not followed up because the horses could not be called upon for the further exertion which the Boers were able to get out of their horses.

'Hotspur,' in December, 1903, writing of a meeting at Sandown Park, says, in the *Daily Telegraph*, that 'the field was constituted of a typical collection of chasers.' What could that field be typical of but the general deterioration? And in the same month he says that Lawyer III. was an awkward customer to ride, for he overpowered his jockey in the preliminary, and in the actual race he pulled so hard that he began to brush through his fences! Perhaps that is not the only lawyer that is an awkward customer! And on December 28, 1903, in supporting Lord Stanley's animadversions on early two-year-old racing, he uses expressions which clearly prove serious general deterioration. He speaks of the paucity of stayers now in training. He says that Cup horses of the approved type of Isonomy or Isinglass are seldom met with; that the purely old-fashioned sort of thoroughbred, such as Fisherman, exists, apparently, only in the records of antiquity. He cites Mr. Chapman as to the few old horses there are in training of sufficient class to compete for the big prizes at Ascot; speaks of the tendency to breed so many weeds, and of the overwhelming progeny of worthless sires with which England is overrun. He affirms that short races are doing incalculable harm to the breeding of sound racehorses, and that the strenuous desire to make the game pay overrides any laudable hope that the highest and best attributes of our thoroughbreds may be solidly maintained. He follows this up the very next day in speaking of a race-meeting at Wolverhampton, with the statement that, generally speaking, the competitors were of poor class, and that extended comment would be useless.

Sir Walter Gilbey, in the *Live Stock Journal* Almanack, 1903, says that the decline in horse-breeding in England still continues. And Sir P. Albert Muntz, Bart., in the same work for 1904, says that there are nothing like the number of good stout, well-bred horses with good limbs and feet that there were formerly, in which opinion he thinks he will have the support of the majority of experienced horsemen.

Professor Wortley Axe, in the *Live Stock Journal* Almanack, 1903, says that there is still a widespread disregard of inherited defects, and that stallions abandoned by the more careful breeder find their way into the hands of less scrupulous owners, and at a small fee command large patronage. And in the same journal Mr. C. Stein writes that ordinary purposes are served by the sale of the failures.

It has been lately stated in an eminently first-class and influential Australian newspaper of exceeding fairness that Mr. Adye readily acknowledges that horse-racing has improved the breed of horses, and that that proposition is, of course, unquestionable, since it is only through the instrumentality of the turf that the blood of the thoroughbred has been kept uncontaminated.

Then a statement of Mr. Adye's is quoted that 'not a hunter . . . but owes the best of his qualities to some one or other of the pure-bred sires with which the Stud-Book teems.'

The first of these statements does not put exactly Mr. Adye's words; the second is, of course, the writer's statement, and not Mr. Adye's; but altogether these statements do not quite precisely represent Mr. Adye's views. Mr. Adye's statement is that the influence of the turf has been beneficial as regards the improvement, not because of the horse-racing simply, but entirely because of the introduction of Eastern horses, several of which he names. Further, Mr. Adye's reference to pure stallions in the Stud-Book appears to me to refer to the pure Arabs imported, and not to the general pure-bred English thoroughbreds, as the newspaper account might lead the reader to suppose.

I refer to this newspaper statement because if, in such a leading paper, it would seem to appear that the writer has misapprehended what Mr. Adye really says, so that what he says of the Arab reads in favour of the English-bred horse, how much more likely is it that dandies, jockey-boys, and fair forms, excited by the gambling demon, should be mistaken!

Mr. Adye bears strong witness to deterioration. He says that 'nine-tenths of English horses are hopelessly and helplessly used up before reaching maturity ; that then they are sent to the stud, which is flooded with speedy broken-down crocks and jades, nervous and irritable in temper, their constitutions impaired, and joints and ligaments strained and injured by the severity of their early training.'

Then he gives his final and deliberate opinion that though at one time the effects of racing seem to have been distinctly advantageous, yet now that it has become a business it appears to have ceased to be of use in that direction. Is it reasonable, in the face of the evidence I have given in this chapter, to crack up racing as tending to improve the thoroughbred ?

A few observations of 'Hotspur's' in the *Daily Telegraph*, on different dates, regarding different meetings, may be taken as signs of the times :

November 17, 1903 : 'The runners . . . were much of a muchness, and the fact that the winner was entered to be sold for 50 sovereigns was a significant commentary on the calibre of the opposition.'

December 29, 1903 : 'Generally speaking, however, the competitors were of poor class, and extended comment would be useless.'

December 30, 1903 : ' The character of the sport was somewhat mediocre so far as the quality of the actual competitors was concerned.'

January 2, 1904 : 'Generally speaking, the character of the competitors was exceedingly moderate. . . . The field was disappointing.'

And again: 'Florio Rubattino was in a measure tarred with the same brush as Salvador, who utterly disgraced himself.'

January 4, 1904: 'Lord Bobs was a sprinter of exceptional ability . . . though the attempt to prove him a stayer as a three-year-old ended in failure. Redcar's lack of stamina was here very distinctly exemplified.'

January 6, 1904: 'The running gave rise to caustic criticism, which I am bound to believe was in the majority of cases perfectly justified.'

And again: 'The moderate Vogelkop scored somewhat easily.'

January 15, 1904: 'Generally speaking, the quality of the greater portion of the animals entered is singularly bad.'

And again: 'The Haydock Park Steeplechase did not attract a very gay lot to the post. The hopes of the Irish division were centred entirely in Little May II. She, however, ran very disappointingly.'

January 26, 1904: 'Reinforcements in the shape of new blood are very much needed.'

And the same writer, in 'Notes and Anticipations' in general (date mislaid), writes of the paucity 'of stayers now in training'; that 'the purely old-fashioned sort of thoroughbred, such as Fisherman, exists, apparently, only in the records of antiquity'; of 'the tendency to breed so many weeds'; of 'the overwhelming progeny of worthless sires with which this country [England] is overrun.' And he affirms that 'short races are doing incalculable harm to the breeding of sound racehorses'; that 'the strenuous desire to make the game pay overrides any laudable hope that the highest and best attributes of our thoroughbreds may be solidly maintained.'

February 9, 1904 : 'Although there were plenty of runners, they were of poor class . . . a fair sample of the everlasting crocks.'

February 10, 1904 : 'The quality of the competitors was singularly bad, with few exceptions.'

February 12, 1904 : 'A very indifferent lot to beat.'

February 13, 1904 : 'None of those who ran except two have been regarded seriously.'

February 17, 1904 : 'The business was singularly tame, owing to the weakness of the fields. Not even increase of stakes can provide a panacea for the painful deficiency in workable material.'

It is no answer to 'Hotspur's' observations to say that there are some good horses. The merits of a breed for use does not depend on the quality of the few; it depends on the general quality of the many, of the breed as a whole, which, except as to the very few, seems from the accounts of everyone to be sadly wanting.

I very much question whether, in all the books that have ever been written about the horse, from the Christian era down to date, you can find so many contemptuous criticisms of the pure Arab as those I have culled from 'Hotspur' alone in a few short weeks concerning the boasted English thoroughbred; and I should as greatly question whether all the praise that has been lavished on that thoroughbred since he has been set up as a thoroughbred and put in a Stud-Book is equal in weight or authority to the one short panegyric of Job on the Arab, poetical though it be.

After the greater part of this work had been sent to England for printing, I read in the *Quarterly Review* for January, 1904, some remarks strangely corroborative of what I have written. The writer scoffs at the idea that racing improves the breed of horses. He affirms that the facts about the Remount Department cannot be considered by the most resolute optimist as providing the slightest ground for the belief that a useful national breed of horses has been fostered by the turf. He affirms (as I have above affirmed on the authority of our old and respected Australian bookmaking friend, Mr. Joe Thompson) that in the art of producing a staying thoroughbred France is our superior. He speaks of horses trained only to scramble off from the starting-gate on their toes, and scurry over a few furlongs, in which the advantage of the start is everything. He points out that Isinglass was asked to carry silk—I suppose that means to race—only twelve times in four years; that Persimmon's winnings were the result of only nine races, Flying Fox's of only eleven. Indeed, he shows it is much worse than I have above depicted it, or even imagined, for he states that, out of the enormous number of English thoroughbreds foaled in 1900, only seven were good enough to go to the post and oppose a French horse in the last Derby, and the French horse beat six of them. He denounces the modern Turf and breeding as 'hysterical money-juggling,' and he adds to the hints that I hereafter respectfully vouchsafe to Governor Sir George Clarke and others by the severe sentence : ' The greater the names of those who stand highest in the racing world, the deeper is the scandal that they should leave untouched the plague-spot which contaminates the whole.'

The *Australasian* (January 30, 1904) quotes the *Field* as stating that in sober truth the Turf, viewed from the standpoint of its mission to improve the breed of horses, does not advance, rather does it retrograde, and that the winning of valuable handicaps is no criterion of blood, the bottom weight being more likely than the top weight to win. That means, of course, that the worst horse is more likely to win than the best horse. Is that likely to improve the breed ?

There is a book, written in 1901, ' The English Turf : a Record of Horses and Courses,' by Charles Richardson. It is written in a very fair spirit, and I should say likely to become a classic on the subject which it deals with. What the writer does not know on races and racehorses, and racecourses and racing training, is evidently not worth knowing.

DETERIORATION OF THE HORSE IN ENGLAND 47

He does not approve of sprinting. He describes many, perhaps a majority of sprinters as high on the leg, too short from shoulder to quarters, narrow, split-up, and short of bone, which he naïvely enough says are not the sort of horses to breed. He complains of the breeding from roarers, and states that, though a roarer may produce a great horse, he also sires many worse roarers than himself, and he is inclined to think that roaring is greatly on the increase. Of course it must be if you breed from roarers!

He says that it is quite a common thing to see up to half a dozen horses in one afternoon's steeple-chasing with the tube after tracheotomy in their throats. I had no idea when I began these papers that things were as bad as that. He says that stamina is greater in the Eastern horse than in the breeds indigenous to any other country, and that the thoroughbred, where he has stamina, gets this quality from his Arab ancestor.

On a deputation, March 8, 1904, to Lord Onslow, President of the Board of Agriculture and Fisheries, Lieutenant-General Sir John Freyer stated that, as a purchaser of remounts for the army for many years, he found that 80 per cent. of the horses presented were unsound. That is a very recent authority for deterioration in England. Will anybody dare say that a similar percentage of English horses were unsound fifty years ago, when the influence of the Arab was more recent and direct? Eighty per cent.! Are not those authorities justified whom I shall quote in my next chapter, and who scoff at the idea that racing improves the breed of horses?

Mr. Robert Black, in his 'Horse-racing in England,' writes that the object both at home and abroad appears to be, not the general improvement of horses, but rather the production of a phenomenon and the performance of some wonderful deed. The wonderful deed referred to is, of course, not weight-carrying, or exhibition of docility, or staying power, or usefulness as a hack, or ability to go through a campaign like Abder Rahman's Arab did, but the ability to sprint. Sprinting is very wonderful, and it gratifies the trainer, the jockey-boy, and the gambler.

Is it a wonder that in March, 1904, at the meeting of the National Council of the Evangelical Council, 'Ian Maclaren' denounced the craze for sport, and asked, 'Was there ever any such cant as to defend horse-racing because it secured a good breed of horses?'

Lord Durham complains of 'weediness' of English horses (*Mail*, December 5, 1898).

Sir Walter Gilbey, in the *Nineteenth Century*, June, 1904, states that the most important departments of the industry of horse-breeding have never been in a condition so grave as they are to-day, and that the decline in the number of horses of the useful class suitable for military purposes has been manifest for years past. The racehorse as a racehorse is hardly worth considering as an asset in the national defence.

DETERIORATION OF THE HORSE IN ENGLAND

When the Duke of Wellington, at a Waterloo banquet, said that the French were the best cavalry in the world, Colonel Taylor explained to General Sebastiani that the English were brave, but could not hold their horses; they passed through, and were then taken in the rear. That cannot be the fault of the men, who are as strong as the French; it must be the fault of the horses, the temper which the style of breeding and impure crosses have developed.

This temper is accounted for by Mr. J. H. Sanders, a great American authority on the horse, in a recent book which he has published. He claims various improvements as brought about in the thorough-bred, yet states that, having for generations been bred with especial reference to racing, he has acquired peculiarities of temper that render him undesirable for the more sober, steady uses of every-day life, and that the course of breeding has made him too nervous and excitable for ordinary business uses. Mr. Sanders has before pointed out that infirmities of temper were especially liable to be transmitted.

This was illustrated at a review at North Baddlesby (September 3, 1904), where a horse of the 8th Hussars broke its leg and was shot, and the noise induced a panic among 500 horses, which rushed and were badly injured, causing a stampede on the part of 500 other horses; seventy rushed to Winchester, whose streets they traversed, and 200 to Southampton, where they plunged into the sea. Some were drowned, twenty were killed, and 200 were missing.

There was further illustration during a series of military manœuvres near Kildare, September 18, 1904, when 600 horses stampeded and seriously injured four sleeping troopers. Many of the animals were also hurt. It may be safely assumed that there was more or less thoroughbred blood in every one of these horses. Mr. Henry Custance, the great jockey, gives a further illustration (amongst others) in the case of the stallion Broomielaw, 'who transmitted his bad temper to most of his progeny.'

For the benefit of the gentleman known in Australia as 'Wapstraw,' I put in Appendix I. a summary of the criticisms upon the English race-horse, many of them from racing men.

CHAPTER IV

CAUSE OF DETERIORATION

THE cause of deterioration is the same in Australia as in England, and has been several times referred to by many of the authorities above mentioned. Rudyard Kipling has 'spotted' it. It is 'sport.' Sport has permeated society, and is ruining England (*vide* the *Quarterly* and *Blackwood* for January, and *Macmillan* for February, 1904). The same craving for sport which gives us the 'flannelled fools at the wicket or the muddied oafs at the goals' has brought about a ruin of horse-flesh which is appalling. 'The officers in garrison at Ladysmith before the war played tennis instead of studying the topography of the country' (*Quarterly Review*, July, 1902). Nero fiddled while Rome was burning.

Sport has become in a large degree the be-all and the end-all of horse-breeding. As Mr. Tom Mann observes (*Adelaide Observer*, October, 1902): 'Too much interest is shown in the pedigree of a "gee-gee," the qualities of a "gee-gee," and which "gee-gee" should be backed.'

There must be 'something' in it when the great poet and the great Socialist agree.

Lord Curzon of Kedleston follows suit, and is evidently alive to this terrible weakness of his countrymen. He called attention to it in his great speech at the Guildhall when receiving the freedom of the City of London, July 28, 1904. He was diplomatic in his language, which was none the less impressive on that account.

'You have only to look,' said he, 'to the newspapers to see that, with rare exceptions, the average Englishman is much more interested in the latest football or cricket match, in a motor trial or in a wrestling encounter, than in the greatest responsibility' (the government of India) 'that has been undertaken by his countrymen on the face of the earth.'

Is it a good thing for a country that that could be said of it? I wonder why Lord Curzon forgot horse-racing?

Kipling also says, 'You train your horses and the dogs you feed and prize,' and that is done till little is thought of except training in order to gamble. The horse is not valued for his usefulness, but for his lack of usefulness; not for the real work he can do, but for his ability to run one or two short-distance races, even if he then perish, as indeed he often does. In all animal nature, if you highly develop one quality, that is inevitably developed at the expense of some other quality. The horse is no exception. All along the line the mischief has increased, is increasing, and ought to be diminished. The papers are full of eloquent descriptions of the racing establishments, of 'lovely yearlings' by celebrated sprinters, and of the odds and the doubles. Our farmers' sons in Australia, many of them, don't stick to the plough, but look to visiting their best girl on some 'thoroughbred' whose sire has won a Muggletonian Handicap or whose grandsire was a useless thousand-pounder, 'not worth sixpence.'

Our collegians of seventeen worship and revere our jockey-boys of fourteen and fifteen and the stable-lads of thirteen who can give them 'a tip.' The knowledge of most of the rising generation as to horses is sucked in from infancy from such sources as this, almost with their mother's milk. It is only natural that they should look upon 'the crooked-legged, deformed brute,' that Mr. Day speaks of, as perfection. I know instances where stable-boys have given 'the tip' to school-boys, who have given it to their mothers, who have passed it on to the fathers, who have then lost their money on the 'tote.' I was told of one case recently where a child of five was given a shilling to put on the 'tote.' Young ladies—the future mothers—talk of the favourite and the totalizator, and know much more about the double than they do about the Psalms of David, and the housemaid wants to know which horse to back for the Cup. The barmaid becomes a very high authority indeed, and if her 'best boy' have a relative in a racing-stable, she becomes for a week or two of greater importance and celebrity than Her Excellency the Governor-General's wife.

Mr. J. Snowy, a betting gentleman who has, he says, spent all his lifetime in travelling between England and Australia and India, and so gained the title of 'The Stanley of the Turf,' writes in his book of 'the glorious country called Australia, where every man, woman, and child takes an interest in the great Melbourne Cup, and where 90 per cent. of its inhabitants are born gamblers.' Is this betting gentleman wrong ? Then let us inquire of religion and piety. The Rev. W. G. Maconochie, at the Session of the Presbyterian Assembly in Melbourne (*Register*, November 15, 1902), said that Australia was the paradise of the Spieler, tote, and the bookmaker and all that class, and that there were many people who could speak of nothing but horses throughout the year. The reverend gentleman scarce meant Suffolk punches. Of course he meant beasts to gamble with—living machines largely used to fleece the unwary. We thus find the poet and the Socialist, the preacher and the sportsman, all concurring. Later on they have been supported by the leader of the Labour Party in South Australia: 'Gambling was eating the vitals out of the working classes. Betting on horses was the growing curse of South Australia.'

The 'vets' unwittingly but necessarily aid in the degeneration. Doctors live by the sick, not by the sound. So with 'vets.' I am sure that 'vets' as well as doctors do their level best when consulted. I gladly trust them both, but they cannot be expected to complain of, however much they may regret, those decrees of Providence which bring about sickness in men, or of those practices of men which increase it in horses. Farming horses don't often need a 'vet,' and the healthier a horse is, the less, of course, the 'vet' knows about him, the less necessity there is for his being doctored, the less necessity for the 'vet.' And Arabs do not much need a 'vet.'

But the 'spavined, ringboned, roaring creatures, leggy and deficient,' which so many complain of, can only be kept running by the aid of 'vets.' Is it any wonder, therefore, that the 'vets' get to adopt the views of the racing men, that the spavined, roaring, sickly thoroughbred is the best horse in the world? So he certainly is—for the 'vets.' Their business is to physic and cure sickly horses. If there were no sickly horses, there would be none to physic or cure.

I dare say that, from the 'vet's' point of view, 'the Arab is a failure.' Mr. Blunt publicly stated at his sale (August 14, 1901) that his veterinary surgeon's bill for the year amounted to only £5 3s., a fraction over a shilling a head. The Boer burghers did not breed for sprinting; they didn't much need 'vets.' If they had, De Wet would have been caught two years before he was. The Boer bred for use, and consequently laughed at us. Should not that be a lesson? I recognise, as well as the racing men, that a sound, good thoroughbred, when you can get him, is a grand animal, and is very useful for breeding purposes. But that is on condition that he is judiciously used, and still more that he is 'judiciously' selected.

No farmer who breeds for use can compete in price with the racing man who breeds to race, and who will run the price of his nimble-footed sire up to £20,000 or £30,000 for racing purposes, and who will demand 100 guineas to 300 guineas for the services of a sire, or even 500 guineas or 600 guineas—for it has run up as high as 600 for Flying Fox. He may be worth that for gambling, but what farmer can breed or buy at these prices? It stands to reason that, if the farmer breed from English thoroughbreds, he must put up with the inferior sires, and therefore that the offspring must be inferior. The offspring of such a sire would be inferior even if given the best blood mares; how much more inferior, therefore, from cross-breeds and cocktails!

It could not be expected to be—it could not possibly be—otherwise than that there should be deterioration. There are, I think, about 5,000 horses named in the Australian Stud-Book of 1897, probably now many more, very many of which are stallions. There has been but one Carbine. What is to be done with the failures? If a breeder can get £50 or £60 by selling a failure for use as a stallion, he cannot be expected to geld him in order to get £10 or £15 only. Why should he? But he gets entered in the Stud-Book, and he gets bred from. Would it be any wonder if the thoroughbred should be deteriorating in rapidly increasing progression? Indeed, the more screws there are in the world outside the select blue-ribbon few, the more valuable those select few become, because the more certain to win races. The more valuable the select few become, the more, of course, is the general breeder driven back upon the failures.

The consequence of all this racing and gambling has been that racing men, betting men, horsey 'swells,' 'the girl of the period,' and the rising generation of young men and maidens, all preach racing and make the Stud-Book their study, and most of them have practised gambling on races, so that nobody has been left to say a word for anything but the sprinter. A screw on a leg and a half, cow-hocked, spavined and a roarer, has been magnified by the 'ten-dollar amateur' of the London *Times* as something supernatural because he is entered in the Stud-Book, and for no other reason, albeit that that book itself is an authority for the fact that, in Australia at least, many of them are not worthy of entry. How many are? Sickly quadrupeds who ought to go to the knackers are worshipped and admired because they are called thoroughbreds, and are used by the thoughtless and the ignorant to the discomfiture of all who wish to see good and useful horses. A farmer will pay thirty shillings for the use of a legless bag of bones under the name of a thoroughbred because he has been taught all his life that the thoroughbred is perfection, when he will not give two or three pounds for a useful sire.

The disease has taken root in Canada, where it is said that, instead of encouraging and patronizing the best sires, they prefer to use any kind of a brute at half-price—the old story, penny-wise and pound-foolish.

Mr. C. B. Fisher tells us Australians that the intention of racing was to improve the breed of horses, but that that certainly is not the case now, as sprinting horses lack stamina. I do not think that that was the intention of racing. The intention was to have some sport. But if it really were the intention, it sadly fails of being carried into effect, yet when a clergyman denounces racing as leading to gambling, he is told, 'Oh, but racing is necessary to improve the breed of horses,' and people pretend to believe it. They actually did believe it thirty years ago. But nobody believes it now. Everyone knows to the contrary. Mr. Fred Adye, in his book on horse-breeding (1903), says that while he believes there was an honest desire to improve the breed by those who first introduced racing, 'yet that any such commendable motive animates and inspires any considerable portion of it, and particularly the ignoble army of welshers, gulls, loafers, and tipsters, who frequent every racecourse in the kingdom, is manifestly incredible.' How many thousands of the best men of England were killed or wounded by the breakdown of weedy horse-flesh in the Transvaal no man will ever know. Verily are my sons who were there justified in considering themselves lucky to have got through safely.

The reason why worthless sires are largely used in horse-breeding is mainly because of their cheapness; they are cheap because they are useless: their cheapness comes because they are not of much use. 'Bruni' says in the *Australasian* (September 15, 1900) that palpably we are doing our best to encourage sprinting, and we therefore do not hesitate to breed from hereditary non-stayers, sire and dams.

'Faneargh,' in the *Sydney Mail*, April 26, 1902, writes that the class of horse at present bred is unsuited for army requirements, and that much of this is due to the sorry specimens called thoroughbreds which travel the country at a very cheap fee, which fact alone induces farmers and others to make use of them rather than an infinitely better animal at a slightly increased fee. Horses like Carbine, Gang Forward, and Fisherman, don't travel.

G. S. Singleton, in the *Australasian*, October 25, 1902, says that the craze for racing in Australia had undoubtedly more to do with the degeneracy of our saddle-horses than all other causes combined, and that the long-limbed pampered weed, being no longer fit for racing, is bought because of his pedigree by some ignorant breeder who expects to raise saddle-horses. In other words, they sell the screw to the poor breeder, and then they laugh at him for being ignorant, and the 'poor ignorant breeder' goes his way rejoicing. Yet the poor fellow is not entirely to blame, because till South Africa was discovered there was none to show him the contrary.

Mr. De Vere Hunt speaks of weeds and wastrels as fostered for speed at short distances under light weights, so that for one sound weight-carrying and long-running racehorse an abnormally great number of unsound, weedy half-milers or four-furlong shadows can be polled. Even Mr. Day, who at times so cracks up the English thoroughbred, says that 'wiseacres prefer to breed from a stallion that has been parted with chiefly on account of disease, or a defect which really renders him quite unfit to be a sire.' That sentiment is very emphatically verified, as above mentioned, by the statement in the Australian Stud-Book that many of the Australian-bred sires are not worthy of entry. No wonder if Mr. Day be right!

An article on colour in horses in the *Australasian*, January 14, 1899, incidentally states that the short-distance handicaps are believed by many horse-breeders, and he thinks with much reason, to be the cause of the falling off in the thoroughbred. How gingerly it is put—'are believed'! Again I say, Why, they know it. Mr. Adye says that it is no exaggeration to say that nine-tenths of our racehorses are hopelessly and helplessly used up before maturity. I shall again refer to Mr. Adye.

Mr. W. H. Lang says that it is evident that horse-racing is not improving our breed ; that two years ago he wrote to that effect, and that things are quite as bad now, or a good deal worse, because we do not hesitate to breed from hereditary non-stayers, sires and dams.

Mr. Adye advises his readers not to breed costly exotics, and says that breeding for size results in a huge overgrown brute, soft and clumsy as a rule, and nearly always deficient in quality and character.

Mr. J. I. Lupton, F.R.C.V.S., in his book on the horse (1881), says that the cause of deterioration is racing, that it causes deficient stamina, militates against producing stout stallions, and that it is strange that English intellect should be absorbed in breeding such horses. He states that nineteen out of every twenty colts are unable to withstand the ordeal of training.

Sir George Chetwynd, in his racing reminiscences, says that the enormous number of two-year-old stakes has to answer for sad deterioration, and year after year foreigners come over and buy our soundest horses for stallions and our best mares for brood mares to an extent which is positively distressing. Mr. Day writes that out of forty-six runners only six carried 8 stone 7 pounds or over, while forty carried less weights down to 5 stone 7 pounds. But disheartening as such a discovery is, it is positively pleasurable, he says, when contrasted with Newmarket, where in three handicaps, out of seventy-six runners, only one solitary horse carried above 8 stone 7 pounds, while seventy-four carried a less weight down to the minimum. Were these the wretched creatures to run down De Wet? Were these the boasted English thoroughbreds? I may remark in passing that it seems to me rather a funny way of improving the breed, to penalize the best horses by handicaps. I should rather think that the best horses should be encouraged. But, really, improving the breed is the last thing thought of.

Mr. Burdett-Coutts, M.P., in his preface to 'The Brookfield Stud in 1901,' challenges the exclusive use of the thoroughbred for light horses, and writes on the tendency of such sires to get long-legged and weedy stock. He adds that it was time that the industry of horse-breeding should shake off the silken chains of sport and caprice, and don the sober garb of an economic pursuit. Mr. William Day caps this by saying that 'such was the rage nowadays for fashion, that dwarfs or giants, legs crooked or straight, are alike quickly bought at any, even enormous, prices, often to their new owners' sorrow' ('Racehorse in Training,' p. 126). One can hardly help feeling sad: 'dwarfs or giants, legs crooked or straight'!

Of course, the public craze and folly spoil the jockey-boys, and Mr. Day fears that the Education Act will still further elevate the ideas of both men and boys, who are already too prone to think themselves above their work. Certainly the education of the boys will the better enable them to teach the girls their gambling and horse-breeding notions. But it does not want any Education Act to spoil boys that are beset all day long, whenever they are out of sight of their masters, with requests for 'tips,' and who in exchange 'get well tipped' for their information, be it good or bad. It is greatly from such sources, highly developed during many years, that the fable spreads that the thoroughbred is a pure and independent breed of horse-flesh.

I desire emphatically to say that I express no opinion whatever as to the accuracy of the statements of the reverend gentleman to whom I have referred, or of others that I shall presently cite, as to the alleged evil actions of some of the King's subjects in respect of racing. My readers must judge of that for themselves, for I claim no authority in this matter. I have never had the value of a penny on a racehorse, and have only been on a racecourse four times in my life. All that I assert is that there is much betting, and that that and sprinting are ruining the thoroughbred.

I have no prejudice against the thoroughbred or against races. I own one or two thoroughbreds, have raced one or two, won a race with one of them, have owned two or three others which have won races, and I have bred two or three more. I do not belong to the Salvation Army, and I do not want to rival the parson; but I cannot help seeing that as sprinting has ruined the breed of horses, so is it helping to ruin the nation by developing an idle, gambling spirit, in doing which it increases the deterioration of the horse. Ten years or more ago, Mr. Goschen (now Lord Goschen) warned young Englishmen to check their love of sport, and pointed out that it was that which enabled the studious young German to beat the Englishman in the race for life; and so recently as September 8, 1903, the *Times*, drawing a contrast between the American young men who had flocked to the new wheat-lands of Canada and 'the ten or fifteen-dollar amateurs from the old country,' pointed out that the fallacy was still much in favour in some parts of England and Scotland, ' that an athletic young man who wears gaiters and riding-breeches on all occasions was necessarily qualifying himself to be a successful colonist.' Under the influence of the racing gamble, the Australian young man is tending in the same direction, if, indeed, he has not already beaten his English contemporary. These youths, of course, affect to be horsey, which is the reason why they wear gaiters and breeches.

After I had written most of the above, a Governor gets into print by way of corroborating me on this —a great Governor, too. And in corroborating me he corroborates the Socialist and the Poet, the Parson and the Sport, above referred to. It is pleasant to be corroborated by a Governor! The Melbourne telegram in an Adelaide paper of October 16, 1903, states that Governor Sir George

QUAMBI STUD FARM, MOUNT BARKER SPRINGS, SOUTH AUSTRALIA.

Clarke, no bookworm or goody-goody, but a military man of high reputation, says: 'That there is far too much betting in Australia, that betting encourages the spirit of gambling, and that that spirit must exercise a most demoralizing influence in many directions.' It has certainly demoralized the thoroughbred. I must say, however, that I rather admire the tender way His Excellency puts it. Betting encourages the 'spirit of gambling.' It always seems to me that betting is gambling. If not, what is it?

But if betting only 'encourages the spirit' of gambling, none the less, according to the words of Governor Sir George Clarke, does it tend to undermine the whole basis of Society. The mode of horse-racing adopted necessarily causes 'sprinting.' Sprinting necessarily causes the breeding of 'sprinters.' The breeding of sprinters has ruined the breed of English thoroughbreds, and another half-century of breeding for sprinting will probably breed it out past redemption. As the breeding of sprinters and 'the undermining the whole basis of Society' go largely together, so the renovation of the English thoroughbred and the preventing of much of the undermining of Society would also go together. *Verbum sap.* As Lord Beaconsfield said, 'I am on the side of the Angels,' I am for breeding a pure breed. And I think Lord Beaconsfield would try to stop the breeding of sprinters. Since writing this, and after it was copied for the press, Mr. Wilfred Meynell's 'Life of Benjamin Disraeli' has appeared, wherein are cited the following remarks of his:

'The British aristocracy, which the multitude idealizes, does not idealize, does not even realize its own status and dignity. The only race your typical noble reflects upon is that run by horses; pedigree and high breeding are concerns only of cattle, his course of study is the racecourse, and the highest homage he offers to the Church is to call a chase after the steeple. And their table talk is stable talk.'

What pleasing unanimity! Tom Mann, the greatest of democrats, and Lord Beaconsfield, the greatest of Tories, at one! Was Lord Curzon tender about treading on the corns of some of the British aristocracy when he forgot to allude to horse-racing?

Happening in the discussion of the question to call the attention of a friend to the above corroboration, by Sir George Clarke, of what I have said as to gambling, which he had not noticed, he called my attention to the singular coincidence that in the same paper as Sir George Clarke's speech appeared there was a corroboration of Sir George Clarke, which I had not noticed, by another very high authority, namely, my colleague the Chief Justice of South Australia, a Baronet and a Privy Councillor of His Majesty the King. This was on the trial (October 16, 1903) of two very young men,

G——, aged eighteen, and D——, aged twenty, for attempting a burglary and shooting a policeman, whom they nearly killed. The Chief Justice pointed out that G—— was released from gaol on September 16, and only three nights later, on the 19th, he shot the policeman. On the afternoon of the day that he shot the policeman he went to the races, having before he went stated that he had two sure things on. At the races he told a witness that he had lost money, and 'would have to pull something down to-night'; and he accordingly engaged in 'the pulling down something'—that is, he attempted the burglary for which he was tried and punished. This is therefore a threefold corroboration — a corroboration of Sir George Clarke's warning as to the evils of gambling, a corroboration of my assertion that 'sprinting' leads to gambling, and a corroboration of my views as to the precocity of Australian youth, illustrated by the readiness of both old men and young to sit at the feet of stable-boys in order to get a 'tip.'

Is it any wonder that this precocity in the babes and sucklings, and this readiness of their elders to sit at their feet for a 'tip,' should develop in them so high an intelligence in a wrong direction that the Chief Justice was led to say that 'the old hands in crime frequently admit that they have been completely outclassed by their more juvenile comrades, whom they regard with mixed feelings of admiration and amazement?

I could not find by the report that the Chief Justice said that 'betting' gave 'a tendency' to gambling. I rather think that he looked upon betting as actual gambling. The gambling spirit led the 'ten-dollar amateurs' mentioned in the *Times* to ape the racing men by wearing gaiters and riding-breeches; the gambling spirit led the young vagabonds sentenced by the Chief Justice to go fresh from the ring to recoup their losses on the turf by 'pulling something down to-night.'

How bitterly the old hands in crime, whom the Chief Justice spoke of as viewing with 'admiration and amazement' the exploits of the young, must bewail the sad dulness of the old times, when sprinting had not so developed as it has of late! Possibly if it were made a misdemeanour to allow the racing of horses less than four or five years old, or races for less than four or five miles, the rapid deterioration of the thoroughbred and of 'the basis of Society' would be alike checked, and there might be fewer 'gaiters' and 'riding-breeches,' and less of our youths of eighteen and twenty going from the betting-ring 'to pull something down to-night.' How would it do to enact that to bet at all on races or 'the tote' or sweepstakes should be misdemeanours?

Races such as, according to Captain Burnaby, the Kirghiz practise on the great Asiatic steppes, from twenty to thirty miles, at the rate of from eighteen to twenty miles an hour, with half-starved horses, might indeed tend to improve the breed of horses. There would be less gambling on races like that. It would, at all events, soon weed out your pampered jades that 'ought not to be in the Stud-Book.' These Kirghiz horses are certainly Eastern, with probably a large dash of Arab blood, for about A.D. 120 the Arabs sent an expedition to Samarcand, and thence into China. In A.D. 206 Abu Kauba, one of the South Arabian Kings, invaded Chaldea, and defeated the Tartars there. The whole of this country has been overrun by Arabs and with Arab horses. What almost certain grounds there are for crediting Arabs with being the cause of excellence to these Asiatic horses will more fully appear in Chapter VII.

The celebrated traveller, Captain Wood, writes that the Tartars were scattered by the Arab sword, and that Islam transformed the face of the continent and established the Mohammedan power by the end of the eighth century almost up to the verge of the Pamir.

Following up Chief Justice Way's observations, the Rev. Mr. Howard, of Adelaide, was driven to say in the pulpit on November 1, 1903, anent the great Melbourne Cup race, that the gambling spirit was not confined to the sterner sex, for many a fair hand would hold the field-glass with trembling grasp because of money staked ; many a fair form would quiver with unwomanly excitement, and many a fair face would betray the influence of the gambling demon's spell. And the Rev. Dr. Bevan, of Melbourne, affirms that racing was making the place a vast gambling-hell, and teaching the little ones and the rising generation that gambling was right. In truth, they suck it in, as I have said before, with their mother's milk. It says little for the intelligence of those of our farmers and breeders who blindly and blandly accept dictation or advice as to what sort of horses they should breed from those who 'make the place a gambling-hell, and deliberately breed for gambling purposes leggy weeds and flat-sided wretches' (Tweedie), 'crooked-legged deformed brutes' (Day), 'little-legged brutes that would fall over a straw' (Day). Of course, our youth having been educated, trained, and brought up with full faith in stable-boys, and in those leggy weeds and deformed brutes, never lose it. That which is indoctrinated persistently in youth becomes a part of the man, as the ecclesiastics well know. 'Catch them young,' they say. These are caught young—very young. This encourages me to attempt a slight *per contra*.

Do 'fair hands,' 'fair forms,' and 'fair faces,' constitute the influence, or part of the influence, with the army to which Sir Michael Hicks-Beach alluded, and which he denounced in a somewhat recent and very mysterious speech? If so, everybody will agree with him. If not, then perhaps many may be disposed to think that it was an unfortunate thing for the Empire that the influence to which he did allude was not more effectual. No influence could be more mischievous than that which sent the 'big hungry chargers' mentioned by Mr. Steevens to be laid up useless in Cairo, and sent similar sort of cattle to be 'expended' by the ten thousand in the Transvaal.

Since Sir Michael's mysterious utterance, the Secretary of State for War has felt it necessary to give warning that the army does not exist for the purpose of providing the men who enter it with facilities for sport. If he possess 30 per cent. of the patriotism of the Japanese, he will see that his precept is carried into practice.

The Rev. Mr. Howard not only, properly enough, denounced the outrageousness of the present racing gambling, but scoffed at the pretence that it improves the breed of horses, a pretence which he stated that the Earl of Derby said was 'a delusion too stale even for jesting.' I say nothing whatever about the ecclesiastical or religious view of the question, but as an Englishman I feel indignant and appalled to know that the nation was all but reduced to a Power of the second class, at a terrible loss of blood, money, and prestige, owing largely to the ruin of the breed of horses by the teachings and influence of the gambling spirit, and, if you are to believe the Earl of Derby, 'to the advent of men who had neither character nor station.' But Prov. xxvi. 11 leads us to doubt whether the advice of the Earl of Derby, Mr. Curr, and scores of other honest advisers, will be more effectual as to horse-breeding than the sternness of the reverend gentleman as to gambling till the time for reaction comes—as, with regard to gambling, let us hope that it probably will come, and, with regard to horse-breeding, as it inevitably must come.

I maintain that the reverend gentlemen who have denounced gambling have a right to scoff when they are told that racing is necessary in order to improve the breed of horses. and I cannot help thinking that they are right when they say that those who patronize racing directly encourage the gambling. Perhaps a few words of Christian exhortation to them might be more profitable than censure. I do not know. The preacher must judge of that. But it is no good to denounce the sinner while he is so largely patronized and supported by the saint. It is useless to denounce the blackleg if Governors and Judges hobnob with him on racecourses. I don't say they do. But the Rev. Mr. Howard, having the courage of his convictions, did say in his sermon that Governors, Judges, and senators were feeding the Frankenstein monster, and plainly imputed to them that they had become law-breakers. Let us hope not.

Severe words. I do not adopt them. I fancy they go rather beyond the occasion. I think they are rather too severe. I desire to express no opinion except as to the deterioration of horses and the cause of it.

CAUSE OF DETERIORATION

Side by side with Mr. Howard's sermon in the newspaper—exactly side by side, in the next column—appears the account of the Derby Day at Flemington. In the one column holy and burning denunciation of all concerned in the show; in the next column a list of the great ones of the earth who patronized the show with their presence! Was that intended by the paper as an illustration of 'Lights and Shadows' of Melbourne life? or was it with the expectation that the names of the sinners enumerated would be a rebuke to the reverend gentleman for his denunciation, or that his denunciation would be a rebuke to the great ones for their presence? In the one column a description of the fair form quivering with unwomanly excitement under the influence of the gambling demon's spell; in the next column the fair form beautifully dressed : cream crêpe de chine, black pleated chiffons, gray voiles, pink and white roses, not to forget toques, and the luncheon and afternoon tea-parties numerous! What a treat for the cynic in this juxtaposition! I have cut out the two parallel columns in order to have them put in a frame. Then we are told that the racing was 'a profitable day's racing to the racing men'!

It is not only in Australia that comment has been made on the influence of fair forms and fair faces. I have read that these have often had too much influence on the War-Office, and through that on war-horses.

To return to Australia, it would appear, according to the preacher, that in order to give 'a profitable day's racing to the racing men' ladies become unwomanly, Governors and Judges almost become lawbreakers, and the most noble animal that serves man is being ruined. I am only concerned here with the latter part of it. I do not judge between the preacher and those whom he was preaching at. Let them fight it out between them. Probably they laughed at him. I have only to do with the ruin of a noble breed of animals. My object is to endeavour to push home the conclusion, to those who really desire to improve the breed of horses, and not to ruin it, that their true interests in this matter are identical with the desires of the preacher. At the same time I must add that I rather think the preacher has the better of the Governor. If the mere spirit of gambling exercises a demoralizing influence in many directions, and tends to undermine the whole basis of Society, I submit that Governors who know it and say it should be chary of giving the chance to preachers to denounce them for encouraging such evils.

I emphatically disclaim any desire in this book to interfere with betting or in any way to denounce betting or betting men. They may bet till they are blind, so far as I am here concerned. They may risk a thousand pounds to a penny as to which sparrow will first hop off a post. My object is to show, on the authority of racing men themselves, that the present style of betting on the present style of racing is fast ruining, if it have not already actually ruined, the English horse.

Supposing that the Governor of Victoria, the Chief Justice of South Australia, and the reverend gentlemen I have quoted, are all of them wrong; supposing, also, that the non-racing men I have referred to are quite in error, it would be difficult to reject the authority of Mr. Day, who shows that almost what may be termed a 'thorough rot' exists in the English thoroughbred. 'Twenty-four out of thirty-six hopelessly suffering from bad feet or defective hocks; unsoundness existing to a great extent; disease in most cases hereditary, and yearly on the increase; roaring and enlarged joints the rule instead of the exception; in no class of horse is mortality so high, of which these are appalling proofs; heavy-shouldered, slack-loined, little-legged brutes that would fall over a straw; crooked-legged and deformed sold for 1,000 or 1,500 guineas, but not worth sixpence.'

If Mr. Day be not wrong, would it not be well for Governors and Judges and senators actively to discourage a system which justifies Mr. Day's statements? Which is the more necessary—that opportunity should be continued for 'many a fair form to quiver with unwomanly excitement, and many a fair face to betray the influence of the gambling demon's spell,' or that no opportunity should ever again be given for enemies riding upon ponies to laugh at

English cavalry, and almost to destroy the Empire owing to the ruin of its horse-flesh? The Legislature has stopped a great deal of gambling, but has not stopped the worst of all—worst because it has that result as well as to undermine the basis of Society. When things have got so bad as Mr. William Day, Governor Sir George Clarke, and the Rev. Mr. Howard show them to be, the Legislature might consider whether it would not be worth its while to go one step further than it has already gone. It will have to grapple with the nettle one of these days if the Empire is to continue a world-power.

If Governors, Judges, and senators, partly out of tenderness towards fair forms and fair faces, do not interpose to check the evil, there is a new great political party coming to the fore in Australia which perchance may by-and-by think it worth while to look into the matter. With the influence of the Churches, that party could cure the evil in a session or two if it chose—if the Churches will really help. If it do, it will remove from Australia the opportunity for such reproaches as that of Mr. Tom Mann or of Governor Sir George Clarke and the Rev. Mr. Howard.

The *Australasian*, February 13, 1904, quotes a successful horse-racer in Canada as saying that, instead of encouraging and patronizing the best sires, people prefer to use any kind of a brute, half-penny-wise and pound-foolish, showing that the causes of deterioration are not merely local, but general. It is much the same in the States; where you find similar results everywhere following the particular course of action, you may be tolerably certain as to what is the cause.

It is significant that *Blackwood's* article of January, 1904—'A Nation at Play: The Peril of Games'—not only denounces the mad craze for sport, but concludes that never was England more formidable in the eyes of Europe than when she was Puritan, and that it was an ascetic Rome whose legions bore down all opposition. *Macmillan* for February has an article on the football fever on the same lines. The Puritanism to which *Blackwood* alludes was not the sentimental Puritanism of the modern Nonconformist Conscience, but the hard-headed fighting Puritanism of Captain Fight-the-Good-Fight and Major Hew-them-in-Pieces-before-the-Lord. If there were more of that kidney now, there would be less sprinting and better horses.

Both those articles in those great publications greatly discount the pretence that sport makes England, and the saying, erroneously attributed to the Duke of Wellington, that Waterloo was won at Eton.

When English workers will neglect work for sport, as *Blackwood* shows—seventy men having improperly left work to see football played, at a loss of 5s. each, with 3s. each costs—things must be rather unsatisfactory. Is there not self-denial enough in the old blood of England—which, after all, must have some weight—to taboo this ruinous craze for sport, and to refrain from helping to make it fashionable, even if the Rev. Mr. Howard, before quoted, be not right in saying that Governors and Judges aid in the gamble ? Is not the old blood of England greatly responsible for setting the example ? Will it not be blameworthy if, knowing what the Earl of Derby, Lord Curzon, Governor Sir George Clarke, and others like them, say, it do not sternly help in the repression ?

We have heard a good deal of the Yellow Agony of late, and Australia is keenly alive to the question, If the opinions of Sir George Clarke and the Rev. Mr. Howard be correct, how will the Anglo-Saxon race be armed to meet the suggested avalanche ? Will the nation which is amenable to their criticism be able to stand up against the weight of a yellow people who, however much they may gamble, none the less do not allow gambling to interfere with their work ?

The *Australasian* (September 4, 1904) quotes the *Sportsman*, that honest men cannot hope to win in the betting ring any more than in playing with a sharper who uses a marked pack ; and also quotes an elaborate defence of racing from the *Sporting Times*, ridiculing 'the nonsense talked of late about the state of the turf,' and, after an elaborate vindication of it, giving an instance to prove the faults of present handicappers, and adding, ' Handicapping of this description is not conducive to honest racing.'

The handicapping complained of had existed for upwards of twenty years, in respect of one owner alone. If such be the turf in its 'higher position,' what of its lowest?

CHAPTER V

THAT THE DETERIORATION HAS BEEN IN FALLING AWAY FROM THE ARAB

Now, what is the deterioration from? I answer, from the Arab. I venture to think that the main stock of the English thoroughbred is Arab in a very much greater degree than is generally supposed, and to a very much greater degree than racing men are willing to admit.

So many people have been led to think that the Arab blood in the English thoroughbred was a sprinkling only, that I am induced to enlarge on this. Indeed, I had myself always adopted that view till recently. The racing men mostly always told me so. But, as I have said, in reality there is now little else than Arab blood in most of our thoroughbreds, except just enough of the 'old Adam' to spoil them and prevent them from being pure. In an article in the 'Horse-breeder's Handbook for 1889-1890,' the writer, Mr. Osborne, refers to the attempts made to acclimatize Eastern blood so far back as the Roman occupation, and shows constant importation of Eastern blood from then down to the present time. He says that Severus is recorded to have held races with real Arabs at Wetherby in Yorkshire before the middle of the second century, and that there is little doubt that similar contests took place at even earlier dates. Severus was a Roman Emperor, and it is notable that he was born in Africa, and in his conquests traversed nearly the whole of the countries of the Eastern horse before he came to England. Possibly these races of Severus in Yorkshire account for the Yorkshireman's love of a horse and skill in horse-flesh, and for his cleverness in racing. The article states that King John was a large importer of Eastern-bred horses, and that further importations of Arabian sires continued during several generations, till interrupted by the Wars of the Roses, after which Henry VIII. took great personal interest in breeding from Eastern sires, his trainer having been styled 'Keeper of the Barra or Barbary Horses.' Cardinal Wolsey held Eastern blood to be of great value, and made extensive use of an Arab sire sent to the King by the Duke of Urbino. Elizabeth had a racing establishment. James I. largely indulged in the sport of racing; his favourite, the Duke of Buckingham, imported the Helmsley Turk, and Lord Salisbury's studs included Eastern breeds. So that even prior to the time of James I. there had been large and long-continued importation of Arab horses to England.

Then it is stated that in the following reign (Charles I.) an important introduction of Eastern blood took place, and many names are mentioned. Soon after Charles II. came to the throne he sent abroad Sir John Fenwick to procure a number of high-bred stallions and mares. Whether Arabs, Barbs, or Turks, they must have been of very high caste, from the improvement which it is stated followed their importation. Many names are given. Even in the short and inglorious reign of James II. one 'Eastern sire of importance was brought to England—the Lyster Turk.'

Similar importation continued in the reign of William and Mary, William importing more Eastern blood. In Anne's reign twenty-four Eastern sires were introduced, and Mr. Osborne gives a list of 175 introduced from the time of James I. till the beginning of the nineteenth century.

Mr. Osborne alludes to the preponderance of the blood of the Godolphin Arabian in Harkaway, and in looking at his pedigree I find the Godolphin mentioned forty-four times. And in Harkaway's pedigree there are also the names of ten other Arabs or Barbs, besides horses which, though not pure Arabs, had much Arab blood—*e.g.*, Eclipse. Of the ten Arabs mentioned in Harkaway's pedigree, there are four of which he has two strains, one of which he has four strains, and one of which he has five strains.

Mr. De Vere Hunt, in his book already cited,

DETERIORATION IS FROM THE ARAB

sums up a chapter on the foundation of the English thoroughbred by a set of conclusions, of which the fourth is that every English thoroughbred is an exotic, coming on both sides from some foreign stock without any cross of English blood. It is very hard to say that there is no English blood at all in him ; indeed, I do not think that is correct ; but Mr. De Vere Hunt says that Roger de Bologne, Earl of Shrewsbury, is recorded to have established 'the race of Spain' about the time of the Conquest.

Now, the race of Spain was Barb or based upon Barbs. After referring to the lightness of the Norman horses at the Battle of Hastings, as compared with the heavier stallions afterwards imported from Flanders by King John, from which he says that our truly noble breed of active dray-horses have sprung, Mr. De Vere Hunt states that it is rather to the introduction in 1121 of such animals as two Arabs which he mentions that we are indebted for a valuable cross. Note this date—A.D. 1121.

Mr. De Vere Hunt also supports the view that there were records of the repeated introduction of Turkish and Barbary horses down to the time of James I., who, he says, not being content with the efforts made to improve the breed through Turk and Barb stallions, dealt with a merchant named Markham for an Arab horse at the then enormous price of £500, although some authorities affirm that the price was less.

He then enumerates some Eastern horses—the White Turk, the Helmsley Turk, the Morocco Turk—which were introduced about that time, and says that one so practically an expert in military matters as the Protector himself had discovered that mere bone and stature were no match against speed, courage, and endurance—in other words, that the big English horse was no match for the Arab. The Protector was no sentimental gushing simpleton. He anticipated the discovery made by Kipling's 'muddied oafs at the goals,' when the Boers laughed at them and their horses, and took them prisoners by thousands.

Mr. William Day also quotes an authority showing an account of the horses of Henry VIII. as including Barbary horses, and says that the importation of foreign horses continued during the reign of Charles I., during the time of the Commonwealth, and also during the respective reigns of Charles II. and James II., and these arrivals, it appears, were mostly from Barbary or Turkey.

Mr. William Day also states that the Arabian horse, like the Turkish, had found its way into Spanish territory, and that the Spanish horse was known in England before the Arabian for improving our breed of racehorses. I do not think that the latter statement is quite accurate, because the merits of the Arabian were known in England before horses came from Spain. But he adds that the reputation of Newmarket for horse-racing seems to have arisen from the spirit and swiftness of the Spanish horses wrecked in the Armada and thrown ashore, and he says that 'most undoubtedly the Arabian or Barb strain gave us, through the Darley Arabian and the Godolphin Arabian, the three best horses known up to that time—Matchless, Harold, and Eclipse, to which three sires all existing thoroughbred strains of most value may be traced, whose blood we find in the three horses which are undoubtedly the best stallions of our time — Touchstone, foaled 1831 ; Voltigeur, foaled 1847 ; and Stockwell, foaled 1849.'

It is recorded that in 1728 the Bey of Tunis sent eight pure-blooded Barbs to Louis XV. of France. Scham was one of them. Roxana was being taken to Highgoblin, when little Scham upset the groom, and conquered and cowed the great white horse. From them came Cade, who fathered Matchem. Scham, now known as the Godolphin Arabian, was also the sire of Regulus, and so down to the best racing stock in England. Even there Scham demonstrated the superiority of blood over bigness, as Saladin did to Kenneth of Scotland, and as the little Syrian ponies did to the great hungry English horses which had to be left behind at Cairo.

In the *Sporting Calendar* for 1770, to which twelve Dukes and no end of other great men were subscribers, there were advertised to stand to cover Matchem, Eclipse and Herod, and ten other stallions described as Arabians—viz., the Khalan Arabian, two Arabians from the province of Yemen in Arabia Felix, Sir Charles Sedley's Arabian, the Damascus Arabian, the Arabian horse Dowla—from the mountains of Moses in Arabia—the Tilfy Arabian, the brown Arabian Lahara, and the chestnut Arabian. Ten Arab stallions publicly advertised engaged at one time in building up the thoroughbred so lately as 1770! Probably there were many more.

According to the reckoning of Major Upton (who wrote another book when Captain), quoted by Mr. Speed in the *Century*, September, 1903, there were used in the formation of the English stud from the time of James I. to the beginning of the tenth century 201 Eastern horses—viz., 101 Arab stallions, 7 Arab mares, 42 Barb stallions, 24 Barb mares, 1 Egyptian stallion, 8 Persian stallions, 28 Turkish stallions, and 2 foreign stallions—all Eastern horses—and these horses worked on a breed improved by the Roman horses under Julius Cæsar, by the Arabs of the Crusaders, by the jennets of the Armada, and by very many lesser importations.

Mr. Speed says that in America, though the popular mind classed all the above as Arabs, they were not so, because the real Arabs were much purer in blood than the others, though the Barbs had virtues by no means to be despised.

Of course, that again opens up the question of Arab versus Barb. My reading induces me to think that they were the same breed, Arab, only differentiated by locality ; but, whether I am right or wrong in that, they both were Eastern horses, of allied breeds, and seem to have been both spoken of by that description, and both were famous. I am satisfied to adopt the view of those who assert that it is really the same breed. If there be any difference, all history except that of Abd-el-Kader places the Arab as the better, as will presently appear ; and if one read carefully all that Abd-el-Kader says, it would rather seem that he was inclined to the same opinion. The reader will therefore please kindly remember that, when I speak of the Eastern horse, I do not do so to differentiate him from the Arab.

It is therefore absurd to suppose, as many do, that the thoroughbred is indebted to only some two or three or half-dozen Arabs for his Eastern blood, by way of lucky accident as it were, when, in fact, he is almost entirely Arab, and the only pure blood that he has got in him is Arab.

Mr. De Vere Hunt further corroborates the statement that at the time of the Restoration Charles II. sent his Master of the Horse with a strong commission to the Levant to purchase stallions and mares, that Barbs and Turkish horses became frequent, that there were numerous imports to

England at this time, and eventually stallions of every breed of the East were grafted on the British horse. He states that the importer of that very celebrated progenitor of our best blood, the Darley Arabian, succeeded in 'establishing' the Arab cross effectually, and in engrafting that race upon the English, and thus completed the working of a system which, under careful management, had given us the desiderata of speed, stamina, beauty, and soundness, up to the period when the result from a new organization of the racing code of laws began to show its sad and lamentable effects upon, not only the highest order of horses, but throughout the various breeds of importance, derived largely from turf blood. I maintain that the Arab breed was partly 'established' before the Darley Arabian, but the point of this opinion of Mr. De Vere Hunt is the ruin caused by sprinting—the new organization of the racing code.

The 'Encyclopædia Britannica' further states that in the ninth year of his reign Edward received from the King of Navarre two running horses, and Henry VIII. imported horses from Turkey, Naples, and Spain. Then what Mr. De Vere Hunt has stated as to Charles II. warmly espousing the introduction of Eastern blood into England, and sending his Master of Horse abroad to purchase, is alluded to, and it is said that it is indeed impossible to find an English racehorse which does not combine the blood of all three—*i.e.*, of the Byerly Turk, the Darley

Arabian, and the Godolphin Arabian, which, in other words, is what Mr. William Day says.

The writer of the article, while giving credit to the native mares crossed from time to time, shows that the powers of endurance and elegant shape of the English thoroughbred are inherited from Eastern horses, most of which were of a low stature. And an account of American trotting horses in the same article shows that there is Arab blood in all the best of these animals, as I shall show by-and-by on the authority of Americans.

Shakespeare was aware of the fame of the Arab. In 'Richard II.' the groom tells the King 'When Bolingbroke rode on roan Barbary.' Bolingbroke was a soldier, and knew. If he had preferred a horse for its hugeness, or only because it could go very fast for a few furlongs, Shakespeare would not have made him ride a Barb. Or if that were only the imagination of the poet, it was founded in Shakespeare's knowledge of history and his assurance that Bolingbroke would have ridden a Barb if he could have got one. He was careful not to mount Bolingbroke on a donkey.

A gentleman of racing proclivities recently mentioned to me, in discussing this question, that on looking into the pedigree of Carbine, as far as it was possible to trace it back, he found that it was so full of Arab blood as to be almost entirely Arab, a remark which induced me to look up the pedigree of some of the old sires, and I find that of almost all of them a similar remark could be made. For example, Eclipse has among his ancestors :

> Hutton's Bay Barb (two strains).
> The D'Arcy Yellow Turk (four strains).
> An old Morocco mare by an Arabian out of a Barb mare.
> Hutton's Gray Barb (two strains).
> Leede's Arabian (two strains).
> The Lister Turk (five strains).
> The D'Arcy White Turk (five strains).
> The Oglethorpe Arabian.
> The Godolphin Arabian.
> St. Victor's Barb.
> The Fenwick Barb (two strains).
> The Helmsley Turk.
> The Chesterfield Arabian.
> Wilkinson's Turk.

Fourteen distinct Arabs, many of them several times repeated, and many of his other progenitors also full of Arab blood.

Again I ask, Is it not, therefore, utterly absurd to pretend, as some people do, that the English thoroughbred is a distinct English breed, with just an occasional infusion of Arab blood, as it were?

I will give another example. Take Whisky, bred by the Prince of Wales in 1789, greatly distinguished on the turf. I find in his pedigree

DETERIORATION IS FROM THE ARAB

seventy-four strains of Arab blood; thirty-four different Arabs are named. He had—

Eclipse (full of Arab blood, as above mentioned).
Herod (full of Arab blood).
Darley Arabian (four strains).
D'Arcy's Yellow Turk (two strains).
Barb mare.
Leede's Arabian (ten strains).
Lister Turk (four strains).
D'Arcy's White Turk (five strains).
Hutton's Bay Barb.
Godolphin Arabian (four strains).
St. Victor's Barb (four strains).
Fenwick Barb (four strains).
Barb mare.
Byerly Turk (five strains).

Curwen's Bay Barb (three strains).
Selaby Turk (three strains).
Morocco mare.
The Newcastle Turk.
An Arab Barb mare.
The Morocco Barb.
Arab Barb mare.
White-legged Lowther Barb.
Morocco mare.
Brownlow Turk (two strains).
Bright's Roan Arab mare.
Bethell's Arabian.
The Harpur Arabian.
Helmsley Turk.
Acaster Turk.
Ogelthorpe Arabian.
Barb mare.
Place's White Turk.
The Pulleine Arabian.
The Byerly Turk.

Thirty-four or more distinct pure Arab ancestors, the blood of many of them several times repeated, as in Eclipse, and many others, even if not, perhaps, entirely Arab, yet full of Arab blood. Yet some people say that there is no good in the Arab!

All the old sires will be found, speaking generally, to be equally full of Arab blood. Mr. William Osborne, as I have mentioned, gives the names of the 173 Arab sires which, he states, were introduced into England from the reign of James I. down to the beginning of the nineteenth century. I have not troubled to take out the pedigrees of the stallions and mares in either of the above pedigrees which I have not specially mentioned as being Arabs, but, as I have said, I think there can be little doubt but that many of them will be found be quite as much Arabian; and then it must be remembered that the English running horse before the time of the Darley Arabian and the Godolphin Arabian or Barb must have been largely Arab.

Web, Whalebone, Woful, Wire, and Whisky, the great family progeny of Waxy and Penelope, bred about 1790, have sixty-eight strains, including thirty-two different Arabs named.

Blacklock, of whom it has been said that no horse in England is a stayer who has not got his blood, has forty-three strains of Arab blood. Touchstone, a comparatively recent horse, bred when racing men were beginning to drop the Arab blood, has got twenty-one strains of recognised Arab blood, and Sir Peter fifty-nine strains of Arab blood. Tramp has fifteen different Arabs mentioned.

I have above once or twice pointed out that Spanish horses had a good deal of Arabian blood in them. All readers of history or travel, or of novels, of the early part of the nineteenth century, have learned this. We have many times in our lives read of the celebrated Spanish jennet. Until very recently, however, I have taken the jennet to mean a Spanish horse of a natural Spanish breed, but it will be seen that the jennet is not really a Spanish horse at all, but an Arabian domiciled in Spain.

The word is not Spanish; it is derived from the Arab word *Jeneta*, a great Berber nation noted for the value of its cavalry. Goldsmith says: 'Next to the Barb travellers generally rank the Spanish Jenette.' In fact, the jennet was a Barb. It was a foundation of fact, and not a dream of fiction, which led Sir Walter Scott, in 'The Talisman,' early in the nineteenth century, to depict Saladin on his Arab, at the end of the twelfth century, riding rings around Kenneth of Scotland's huge charger. That was a preliminary illustration of the folly of hugeness which Oliver Cromwell realized, and which was recognised at Omdurman, and which has since been brought home to the nation, by the Boers. Before the Boer War many did not believe in the possibility of Saladin's achievement. De Wet has now taught them that it was true by illustrating it with examples.

In the old romances which used to be the fashion

before the latter half of the nineteenth century, frequent reference is made to the jennet. For instance, Sir Walter Scott in 'Ivanhoe' speaks of a lay-brother leading for the use of Prior Aymer one of the most handsome Spanish jennets ever bred in Andalusia, 'which,' he says, 'merchants used at that time to import, with great trouble and risk, for the use of persons of wealth and distinction'; and he describes the horses of the Eastern attendants of Brian du Bois Guilbert as of Saracen origin, and consequently of Arabian descent, with fine, slender limbs and small fetlocks, and as forming a marked contrast with the heavy Flanders horses for mounting the men-at-arms. Sir Walter Scott knew better than most men in England what was the history and what was the belief of the age about which he wrote (the end of the twelfth century), and would not have been guilty of an anachronism, and his references show the belief in the Arab which existed at the period he refers to. The Crusaders were men of war—had founded their belief on actual experience. They did not want horses to ride and show off in Hyde Park. If the native breeds had been as good as the jennet, we should not have heard so much of the latter, either in Spain or in England, nor would they have brought them to England at great trouble and risk.

The 'Imperial Dictionary' gives the same meaning of jennet, 'A small Spanish horse, properly "Genet,"' and gives a quotation from Prescott: 'They were mounted *à la gineta*—that is, on the light jennet of Andalusia, a cross of the Arabian.' These Eastern horses are mostly spoken of as Arabian. The same dictionary also gives the statement that the word 'genet' comes from the Berber tribe of Jeneta, who supplied the Moorish Sultans of Grenada with a body of horse on which they placed great reliance. The Moorish Sultans did not value horses for the mere power of half-mile sprinting, nor place great reliance on them for that reason. They wanted war-horses for long and severe wars.

The 'New English Dictionary' has the same meaning and derivation, with several examples, amongst which : ' 1463, item for a genett that my mastyr lent hym in the northe country.' 1674, Milton : ' The Emperor rides in the field with all his nobility on Jennets and Turkey horses.' Prescott : ' Ferdinand Isabella royally attired rode on a Jennet.' Goldsmith's ' Natural History ': 'Next to the Barb travellers generally rank the Spanish Jenet,' which was not unnatural if the travellers were men of experience, because the jennet was almost a Barb or Arab. We must therefore recognise that all the best of the horse-flesh of England throughout the entire history of England is admittedly Arab.

CHAPTER VI

THE EXCELLENCE OF THE ARAB ACCORDING TO MAJOR-GENERAL TWEEDIE, GENERAL DAUMAS, AND THE GREAT EMIR ABD-EL-KADER

I NOW propose to certify the Arab to my readers, first by some quotations from Major - General Tweedie's recent great work on the subject, which are entitled to very considerable weight, because the book is written in a most judicial spirit, giving fully both sides of the question. I do not think it necessary to give both sides fully here; because in this State, at all events, the adverse side has been preached and advocated *usque ad nauseam;* because comparatively little has been said for the Arab; and because I am writing to show that there are great merits in the Arab in opposition to the view of his detractors, who pretend that there are next to none.

Major-General Tweedie has a quotation from Mr. Sydney's book of the horse as to the endurance of the Arab: 'The one quality in which Arabs excel —endurance— and which they share with the Australian horses and Indian mustangs, is not re-

SULEIMAN. ZUBEIR.

quired in civilized States where travelling is either performed by railway or post-horses.'

This is worthy of particular note, because Mr. Sydney advocates the other side, and yet admits the Arab's endurance—that they excel in it. That admission entirely gives away his whole case, so far as regards the question of the best horse for general purposes, and coming from a detractor is particularly noticeable. What is wanted in any civilized country for use is endurance and docility, and especially are those wanted in Australia. And the endurance of Australian horses and Indian mustangs which Mr. Sydney refers to proceeds from the Arab blood, and from the Arab blood only. I am writing primarily to address Australian breeders of other than race and draft horses, and although endurance may not be wanted for the short, light-weighted sprinter or for the 'masher' in the park in a country of railroads, it is ridiculous to tell them that endurance is not wanted in Australia for general use. We have no post-horses, and where are the railroads for travelling in the Bush? Don't we sell horses to India and to South Africa, and is not endurance wanted there?

It is absurd to say that endurance is not wanted in war, and in Australia much profit has accrued by breeding horses for use in war. And much damage has already also accrued to Australia by neglecting endurance in the horses which we have sent away to India and elsewhere.

General Tweedie, after citing Sir Henry Layard in 'Nineveh and its Remains,' who described a chestnut mare belonging to the then (1843) Shekh Sfûk of the Sham mar as one of the most beautiful creatures he had ever beheld, at which they all involuntarily stopped to gaze, states that the Arabian is 'essentially a war-horse; a knight and gentleman to the manner born; a goer-out to meet the armed men;' and he describes the Parthian warfare of the desert, where 'two things make a mare exceptional, the one endurance, and the other the gift of turning and twisting, which distinguishes the Arab horse in India with either a running or a charging boar in front of him.' Even more wonderful than a boar-hunt are the exploits of the Hamran Arabs in hunting the elephant, described by Sir Samuel Baker. Four is the proper number. One of them gallops up ahead of the elephant to tempt him to charge, needing no little coolness and dexterity to keep his horse clear of the charging elephant burning to tusk him, and yet close enough to play into the hands of his fellow-hunters. One of these at the 'psychological moment' jumps off his horse with his drawn sword and hamstrings the elephant. Of course the riders often get killed. This story is endorsed by Mr. Arthur B. R. Meyers, surgeon in the Coldstream Guards, in his book on the Hamran Arabs, and who says, ' It was a great luxury to be mounted on our little horses '—that is, Arabs. How long before the English thoroughbred could be got to be useful in such a hunt? And how would a jockey-boy like to be deprived of his breakfast until he had played the teaser to a charging elephant? And how long before a Hamran Arab could be persuaded to attempt the feat on an English thoroughbred? And how would he be likely to manage if he did?

Many writers have alluded to this extraordinary gift of turning and twisting. Mr. Walter B. Harris, in his book 'The Land of an African Sultan,' describes in two or three places the charging and turning of the Moors. To make one quotation: 'Sometimes the sons of horsemen seemed as if they were charging straight at our tent, and as it was they passed within a few feet of the ropes. Again and again they charged, saluted, fired, and stopped short, after making their horses rear till they seemed as though they must fall back with the cruel Moorish bit.' Contrast this readiness to the rider's wishes with the start of English thoroughbreds for a race!

The London *Times* of January, 1904, in an account of the reception of Lord Curzon, the Viceroy of India, by the Chief of Koweit, on the Arab side of the Persian Gulf, speaks of the cloud of horsemen galloping wildly ahead, hurling their spears, curvetting, pirouetting, and going through all the time-honoured evolutions of an Arab field-day, on their spirited Arab steeds—riders ready to fight on these horses day by day.

Looking back to my stock-keeping days, I used to marvel at the wonderful manner in which my old half-Arab stock-horse used to turn when I was after a bullock, cutting him out or driving him. The old chap was quicker than I was, and quite as quick as the quickest bullock, far quicker than he could possibly have been if he had had to depend upon his rider. He enjoyed the fun, and seemed to watch and anticipate the bullock's movements as a good fencer watches and anticipates the thrusts of his opponent. I believe, indeed, that he enjoyed the fun as much or more than I did, and he seemed to take pride in not being 'humbugged' by the bullock or into overshooting his quarry.

The reader will notice how this turning and twisting would be useful in a polo pony, and the Arab has been spoken of as a 'gentleman' by many critics. General Tweedie then shows how the life of the Arab people tends to stamp their stock with the characteristics proper to a saddle-horse; that everywhere under the sweltering Eastern sun—in Egypt, Arabia, and India—where fast work in saddle or harness is exacted by the masses of the people from their horses, it surprises Europeans how very much better to go than to look at the commonest hacks are. He fortifies the wisdom of the desert as to the advantage and necessity of a horse with endurance by citing Captain Nolan's book on cavalry, in which the Captain quotes Cromwell as on one occasion writing to his Auditor-General that 'if a man has not good weapons, horses, and harness, he is as nought.' A fact which Cromwell well knew. So did the Boers.

If the War-Office had only learned from Cromwell and the Arabs instead of from the pupils of jockeys and bookmakers, and those Piccadilly mashers and Bond Street swells who love to prance about on leggy spindleshanks in the Parks to show off before the dames of Park Lane!

The Major-General reminds us that several of the greatest Generals of modern Europe have shown a strong preference for Arab horses as chargers, and that in the courtly circles of Persia and India this is the horse which is prized above all others, and he affirms that there can be no question that, for one whose seat is not well down in the saddle, the Arabian is the pleasantest and the safest of all the *chevaux de luxe* of the world. He naïvely adds that, as a rule, horses of this breed, when asked to go in one direction, do not insist on going in another direction, or fix themselves on their fore-legs and curl up like hedgehogs, and he relates how, in the brief but difficult campaign of 1856 in Persia, the straight swords and Arab horses of the Bombay Light Cavalry demoralized the Shah's forces, and how chargers from the Euphrates have carried our soldiers to Candahar and Cabul, to Pekin and to Magdala, and how more recently in Burmah, where it is extremely difficult to keep foreign horses healthy, the cavalry of the Hyderabad contingent added to the high reputation which it inherits.

He relates that an officer of the 3rd Lancers of that contingent in Burmah kept ninety of his men constantly on the move for nearly three months without a single sore back, and with but one or two slight girth-galls. After telling his readers what a despiser of Arabs the late Mr. Richard Tattersall was—naturally, for he was a racing man—the General tells us that when a Nedji horse (which he referred to as taken from the Wahabis) arrived in London Mr. Tattersall would not even go to look at him, but nevertheless, on accidentally meeting him, the old man had to declare that he was the finest blood horse of the size he had ever seen. It would be difficult to get more telling evidence.

The General says that it would not be easy to find another breed of horses which is so uniformly distinguished by evenness of temper, gentleness, and willingness, as the Arabian, and that fortitude was as marked a characteristic of the breed as frugality; that the way in which the Arabian will pass through strangles or catarrh and influenza without losing his natural spirit and gaiety is one of his characteristics; that as a racer he is indomitable; that heats are his forte; that he will run two or more races in one afternoon; and that many an Arab racer has continued year after year to add to his laurels, in spite of a thickened suspensory ligament. Not to speak too exclusively of racing, he says that fifty-three years ago Captain Horne, of the Horse Artillery, undertook to ride his gray Arab horse Jumping Jimmy 400 miles in five days, and accomplished the feat on the Bangalore Racecourse before crowds of spectators with three hours and five minutes in hand. Then he denounces bigness, and says that the town Arabs of Arabia, like the 'swells' of London town, admire large animals, and the Turks think that a Pasha ought to be on a horse like an elephant; but the Bedouin Arab knows better, and realizes that the power which the compact little Arabian possesses to carry a heavy man both far and fast is very remarkable. 'Townies' in other places than Arabia seem to like bigness, so as to be 'well up' in the world!

The Major-General quotes Captain Nolan's book on cavalry as containing an account of a Persian troop-horse which, only 14 hands high, was ridden throughout an 800 mile march in India by a private of the 18th Hussars, who weighed with his accoutrements $22\frac{1}{2}$ stone.

At the crossing of the Kistna, a broad and dangerous river, his rider scorned the ferry-boat, and, declaring that a Hussar and his horse should never part company, gallantly stemmed the current in heavy marching order. He contrasts this with a field of Australian horses in a steeplechase in India, which was completely stopped by what they had to encounter. Some fell, others would only jump what they thought proper, and not one passed the judge's box; and afterwards, when their owners were protesting against the course, a battery sergeant-major of the Hyderabad contingent, who happened to be present on his regimental horse—an Arab Galloway—rode him over every obstacle. This paragraph might have been added to the instances mentioned in the chapter as to the deterioration of the horse in Australia.

Major-General Tweedie asserts his claim to practical experience, as he had spent the best hours of a long life in the saddle or on the coach-box, and had marched, on horses of different breeds, from Annesley Bay to Magdala, and from Peshawar to Cabul, as well as over large parts of India, Persia, and Arabia, and had also for several years been Adjutant of a cavalry regiment mounted on Arabs. Then he adds that, if he had not found many sterling qualities in the Arabian, he would not have been so attached to him; and he asserts that in certain circumstances and for certain uses the Arabian horse stands unrivalled. With all his faults, he says that he is such a horse as can never be produced again.

He speaks of a certain Arab horse as 'an Eastern evergreen,' in the possession of General and Mrs. Turnbull, formerly of Calcutta, and then of Brighton, which was brought to England eighteen years before; it was at least twenty-four years old, and to all appearances was as young as ever, especially when mounted.

He explains a peculiarity of the pure Arab, that of sometimes looking as if he were hollow-backed, which, he points out, is not really the case. He shows that Eclipse rose very little on his withers, and was higher behind than before, that in the Arabian also the hind-quarters are frequently higher than the fore-hand, and that in picking Arabs for racing it is not a bad plan to take Eclipse as a model. He points out that the Hon. A. Stewart's famous Arab was a horse whose measurements were 14 hands and $\frac{1}{2}$ inch at the withers, and 14 hands $2\frac{1}{2}$ inches over the loins, for which at first he was more laughed at than admired; but after he had shown his quality all the self-styled judges, as usual, merely said that no one could form an opinion of an Arab. That is the polite way of putting it. In plain language, their eyes have got so accustomed to the weedy, long-legged sprinter that they do not know a true horse when they see him.

Having, so to speak, launched the subject with the opinions of an English soldier who had spent the best hours of his life in the saddle, I propose now to set forth some extracts from a book by a man of another European nationality, also a military man, necessarily free from the idiosyncrasies of an Englishman, and uninfluenced either by goody-goodiness or sport—a stern, hard-headed soldier. It may be his misfortune, but perhaps he never saw a jockey-boy. The title is 'The Horse of the Sahara, and the Manners of the Desert,' and it is written by the French General Daumas, General of a division, commanding at Bordeaux, with commentaries by the Emir Abd-el-Kader.

General Daumas appears to have submitted his opinions to Abd-el-Kader, who wrote the General some letters explaining various Arab views of the horse, and giving Abd-el-Kader's own views and criticisms on the opinions of the General.

It seems to me that the opinions of General Daumas are particularly well worthy of notice, and that the statements of Abd-el-Kader are of more than ordinary interest. No man ever lived who was a better horseman, or knew more about horses, than Abd-el-Kader, and in generalship and statesmanship he was a man of his generation, while the practical knowledge of the French General of Division could not well be surpassed.

Abd-el-Kader was an Arab chieftain, Emir of the Southern Districts of Algiers, of high rank and celebrated for his learning, a great master of horse-flesh and a born leader of cavalry, with the bravery of the Dervishes of Omdurman and the mind and genius of a very great General. He kept the French at bay from 1831 till 1847, when he surrendered. He was of high renown, and I remember him as a great hero in the eyes of the English for many years. He gave the French in North Africa more trouble than General Botha and De Wet gave the

English in South Africa, and, so far as I can recollect, he had no artillery, but only Arab horsemen.

General Daumas reminds us in his introduction that the horsemen of Numidia—*i.e.*, Arabs or Barbs—were famous in the time of the Romans; that Arab horsemen of the present day are in no way inferior to their predecessors; and that the horsemen of Algeria still retain the typical characteristics of both the Barb and the Arab stock. General Daumas spent sixteen years in Africa, during which period he had been entrusted with missions, and had exercised functions which brought him into constant intercourse with the Arabs.

From 1837 to 1839 he was the French Consul at Mascara, accredited to the Emir Abd-el-Kader, after which he was the head of the Arab Office in the Province of Oran, and was finally Central Director of the Arab Office of Algiers. These different posts brought him into close contact with the native chiefs and the first families of the country, and he acquired their language. He says he was determined to find out what was the real value of Arab horses, and what was the nature of the service they were capable of—not by hearsay, but through the evidence of his own eyes; not from books, but from men; and that what he placed before his reader was the result both of his own personal observations and of conversations with Arabs of every grade of life, from the tented chief down to the simple horseman, who would speak of himself in his picturesque idiom as 'having no other profession than to live by his spurs.' He affirms that he had consulted the most esteemed authors and great men of erudition, but confessed that it was among the Arabs that he had met with the most just and practical appreciation of the subject. Surely no man will say that the views of the people which has lived and maintained its nationality by its horses, which has a large literature on the subject, and which are thus vouched for by a French General after close study and long practical experience, are not worthy of being considered?

Then he sets out a letter from Abd-el-Kader, which is, unfortunately, too long to be set out fully here, the more especially as much of it is poetic, like Job's description, so I shall only give a few extracts. When a bookmaker, however hard and practical, having his mind on sprinting, ridicules the Arab opinion of the horse because it is poetical, I crave leave to observe that nobody makes poetry unless the subject be worthy of poetry; men do not write poetry about a pig. And even if men could make rhymes upon the totalizator, it could never be poetry. Discount the poetry as much as you choose, but a wise man will accept the facts which call it forth. Abd-el-Kader writes:

'*To our friend General Daumas. Peace be with you!*'
'Know then that amongst us it is admitted that Allah created the horse out of the wind, as he

created Adam out of mud. What the horse most yearns after is the combat and the race. He is also preferable to the mare for the purpose of war, because he is more fleet and patient of fatigue, and because he shares his rider's emotions of hatred or tenderness. Now, whence come the Arabs of the present day? It is related by many historians that . . . the first man who, after Adam, mounted the horse was Ishmael, the father of the Arabs. He was the son of Lord Abraham, beloved of Allah.

'There was a tradition that some Arabs of the Arzed tribe went up to Jerusalem the noble, to congratulate Solomon on his marriage with the Queen of Saba. . . . Solomon thereupon gave orders to bring from his stables a magnificent stallion descended from Ishmael stock, and then dismissed them. These Arabs on their return home devoted him to foal-getting. . . . This is the stock whose high renown spread at a later period through the whole world. In fact, it was propagated both in the East and the West in the train of the Arabs. . . . Since the introduction of Islamism the Mussulman invasions extended the fame of Arab horses to Italy, Spain, and even to France, where, without doubt, they have left traces of their blood. . . . Invasions transplanted the Arab horse into the Soudan, and justify our asserting the oneness of the Arab stock whether in Algeria or in the East. . . . There remains now only one question to settle with you.

You ask by what outward signs the Arabs recognise a horse to be noble, a drinker of air. Here is my answer : The horse of pure descent is distinguished among us by the thinness of its lips and of the interior cartilage of the nose, by the dilation of the nostrils, by the leanness of the flesh encircling the veins of the head, by the graceful manner the neck is attached, by the softness of its coat, its mane and the hairs of its tail, by its breadth of chest, the largeness of its joints, and the leanness of its extremities. . . . According, however, to the traditions of our ancestors, the thoroughbred is still better known by its moral characteristics than its physical peculiarities. . . . Thoroughbred horses have no vice.' (That, of course, refers to Arabs). 'The Arabs are so convinced of this that if a horse or a mare have given indisputable proof of extraordinary speed, or remarkable endurance of hunger and thirst, of rare intelligence, or of grateful affection for the hand that feeds them, they will make every imaginable sacrifice to get his progeny. . . . The horse carries a full-grown man, a robust cavalier, with standard arms and ammunition, besides food for both, and will go at speed for a whole day and more without eating or drinking. It is by his means that the Arab holds whatever he possesses, rushes on his enemy, tracks him down, or flees from him, and defends his family and his freedom. Let him be enriched with the possession of all that sweetens life, his horse alone is his protector. . . . Do you understand the boundless affection the Arab feels for his horse ? It is only equalled by the services rendered by the latter.'

General Daumas, while frankly admitting that this letter, of which I have set out part, contains an admixture of legendary anecdote with snatches of natural history, sometimes true, sometimes fabulous, says that there are, nevertheless, lurking within it incontestable truths, and that the poets of Greece were inspired by the same idea that it was the wind which impregnated the mares of Thessaly, the swiftest of ancient times ; and it might be that those mares were introduced into Greece from Syria or Arabia together with the fabulous pedigree assigned to them by the poets of both countries. On this General Daumas says that history is in accord with tradition, and that if so the Arabian horses must have been what they still are on their native soil—the fleetest and best in the world. The French cavalry found that out more than once in their history, as did some other cavalry in Africa.

The General says that Ishmael is the personification of the Arab people. The horse had made the Arab King of the Desert, and in return he makes a friend and companion of his horse, and between them there was only one interest. He only desires to add one more word on the portrait of the thoroughbred horse, the pure Arab, by Abd-el-Kader, who takes in at one view, and as inseparable one from the other, both the physical and moral qualities ; and in the General's opinion, as in Abd-el-Kader's opinion, physical qualities alone will never constitute a perfect horse, who must also, by his intelligence and by his affection for the master who feeds, tends, and rides him, unite with him as an integral part.

General Daumas has a chapter on the Barb, of which he had often heard it said that it was very inferior to the true Arabian, and he calls in to act as umpire in the dispute Abd-el-Kader, whose intelligence, whose habits, whose whole life, he says, render him a supreme judge in all matters relating to horse-flesh. This matter has very recently been the subject of discussion in many countries— amongst others, in Victoria, by 'Bruni,' who stoutly maintains that the Arab is not really a Barb. 'Bruni' states that 'the descendants of the Darley Arabian are the winners of nearly all the great races, while the descendants of the Godolphin Barb are gradually disappearing from the front rank of the turf,' and that in all countries the Arab is preferred both for the beauty of form and for superior physical qualities. On this question the remarks of Abd-el-Kader are worthy of consideration.

According to Abd-el-Kader—says the French General—the Barbary horse, so far from degenerating from the Arab, is on the contrary superior to him. But whether so or not, the General is content to oppose to the European horse one identical horse, the horse of the Orient, which, thanks to the French conquest of Algeria, is daily called upon to render to France services more and more valuable and more and more valued.

Then follows another letter from Abd-el-Kader to General Daumas:

'Praise to the one God. His reign above is eternal. To proceed: You have asked us our opinion of Barbary horses, their character and their origin. To give you satisfaction . . . I can do nothing better to-day than send you some extracts taken from the poetical works of the famous Aamrou-el-Kais, who lived a short time before the coming of the Prophet; they refer to the superiority of the horses of the Berbers' (the Berbers took the jennet to Spain). . . . 'Aam-el-Kais was one of the ancient Kings of Arabia who took infinite pains to procure Barbary horses wherewith to combat his enemies. . . . The Berbers' native country was Palestine, whence they were expelled by one of the Kings of Persia. They then emigrated to Egypt . . . crossed the Nile, and spread over the other side of the river. . . . Peace be with you at the end as at the beginning of this letter on the part of your friend,
'ABD-EL-KADER BEN MAHHIDDEN.
'(May Allah cover him with his blessings!)

I think Abd-el-Kader may be wrong as to Palestine being the Berbers' native country; they possibly came through Palestine and Syria viâ Egypt, but were probably Arabs, who overran all those countries, as we know. Besides, the statement in the previous letter rather supports 'Bruni's' view. Dr. Barth explains the connection between the Berbers and the Arabs, and states that the Berbers were a Semitic race, now more or less modified in many districts by intermarriage with the Africans.

After lengthy dissertations on various beauties and qualities of the pure horse, General Daumas tells us that a good horse in the desert ought to accomplish for five or six days, one after the other, distances of twenty-five or thirty leagues, and that after a couple of days' rest, if fed well, he will be quite fresh enough to repeat the feat; and although he says that the distances to be traversed in the Sahara are not always of such great length, yet at the same time it is no very rare occurrence to hear of horses doing fifty or sixty leagues in four-and-twenty hours, and he mentions instances which, he says, will appear incredible, and if witnesses were wanted to confirm the truth of the story, the horses still are alive.

One of a thousand instances—one which was told him by a Zy-ben-Zyan, a man of the tribe of Arbaa —he gives in the relator's words, of which the substance follows:

The Arbaa had some terrible quarrels with the Turks, and agreed to win over by presents of money the Pasha's suite, and to send to himself not merely a common animal, as was customary, but a courser of the highest distinction, which was a misfortune, but the will of Allah, and they were forced to resign themselves.

Then Zy-ben-Zyan continues: 'After the evening prayer my father . . . came to me, and said, "Ben-Zyan, art thou thyself to-day? Wilt thou leave thy father in a strait, or wilt thou make red his face?" "I am nothing but your will, my lord," I replied. "Speak, and if your commands are not obeyed, it will be because I am vanquished by death."'

And when the father sends him off, the narrator continues: 'Without answering a word I kissed my father's hand, took my evening repast, and quitted Berouagnia. . . . I pushed forward for a long time, fearing to be pursued, but Mordjana continued to pull at her bridle, and I had more trouble to quiet her than to urge her on. When two-thirds of the night had passed, and a desire to sleep was growing upon me, I dismounted, and, swinging the reins, twisted them round my wrist. . . . An hour afterwards I roused myself; all the leaves of the dwarf palm had been stripped off by Mordjana. We started afresh. The peep of day found us at Souagin. My mare had thrice broken into a sweat and dried herself. I touched her with my heel. She watered at Sidi-Bou-Zid in the Ouad Ettouyl, and that evening I offered up the evening prayer at Leghrouat.

'These are not journeys fit for your horses,' said Zy-ben-Zyan in conclusion; 'for the horses of you Christians go from Algeria to Blidah—thirteen leagues—as far as from my nose to my ear, and then you fancy you have done a good day's work.'

With regard to this journey, General Daumas in his comments points out that this Arab had done eighty leagues in twenty-four hours; his mare had eaten nothing but the leaves of the dwarf palm, and had only once been watered, about the middle of the journey; and yet he swore to the General by the head of the Prophet that he could have slept the following night at Gardaya, forty-five leagues further on, had his life been in danger.

Zy-ben-Zyan belonged to the great tribe of the Arbaa, came frequently in to Algeria, would tell this story to whoever would listen to him, confirming his narrative if required by authentic testimony, and it was thoroughly believed in by the General. No doubt the General was not as astute and as learned as a boy from a racing-stable; still, a French General of Division is not quite such a fool as to believe every tale which may be told him unless there be reason in it.

In weighing the merits of a thoroughbred of the desert against the merits of a so-called thoroughbred of the racecourse, the worshippers of the latter may affect either to believe a story such as this, and say that their ideal will 'go one better,' or they may affect to disbelieve it altogether; if the former, I say that there is no evidence whatever to induce anybody alive to believe that any racing thoroughbred could do any such journey—I believe he could not—if the latter, I set against their opinion that of General Daumas who thoroughly believed the story, relates other instances supporting his belief; and has had a lifelong practical knowledge and experience.

Another instance that he gives is of an Arab, named Mohammed-ben-Mokhtar, upon whose people a raid was made, with, says the General, 'all the atrocities customary in such cases.' The Arab threw himself on the bay mare, placed one of his children on the saddle before him, and another, aged six or seven, behind him, holding on by the troussequin, and was about to place the youngest in the hood of his burnous, when his wife stopped him, exclaiming that she would not let him have this one, as the enemy would not dare to slay an infant at its mother's breast. Mohammed-ben-Mokhtar, being hotly pressed, travelled all that day and the following night until he reached Leghrouat, where he could rely upon being in safety.

General Daumas gives an instance where, in 1837, an Arab was sent to procure news of the greatest importance, who set out at four in the morning, and returned at the same hour on the following day, having travelled seventy leagues.

General Daumas then says that, to finish with the Barb, and to give, over and above the other qualities he possesses, an exact idea of his strength and spirit, he cannot do better than state the weight carried in most of the French expeditions against the Arabs by the horse of a Chasseur d'Afrique :

	Kilogrammes.	Hectogrammes.	Decagrammes.
Horseman armed and in full uniform	82	—	—
Equipment and pistol	24	—	—
Bread for two days	1	5	—
Biscuit for three days	1	6	5
Coffee for five days	—	6	—
Sugar for five days	—	6	—
Bacon for five days	1	—	—
Rice for five days	—	3	—
Salt	—	—	8
Pressed hay for five days	25	—	—
Barley for five days	20	—	—
Three packets of cartridges	1	3	—
Four horses' shoes	1	6	—
Total (350 pounds)	156	35	13

—156 kilogrammes, or 19 more than the horse of a carabineer, and 26 more than the horse of a cuirassier in France. This weight, of course, decreases as the column proceeds on its march.

And then he asks whether a horse that, in a country often rough and difficult, marches, gallops, ascends, descends, endures unparalleled privations, and goes through a campaign with spirit with such a weight on his back—is he, or is he not, a warhorse? I venture to ask the same question. These weights are hard facts, not poetry. A note by the translator mentions that a kilogramme is equal to 2⅕ pounds, a hectogramme to more than 3½ ounces, and a decagramme is the 100th part of a kilogramme; so that the weight was, therefore, over 25 stone, more than 2 stone in excess of the $22\frac{1}{2}$ stone carried by the little Persian troop-horse mentioned by Captain Nolan, and was not exceptional. Therefore the stories of the Arabs, related with the poetic imagery of an Eastern people, are verified, so to speak, and corroborated, by the business accuracy and actual measurements of a French soldier of responsibility and repute, and the facts of the French General are fortified by the account given by Mr. Steevens of the marching forth of the British cavalry, mounted on Arabs, for Omdurman, as mentioned in Chapter VIII.

There is an Australian work on pure saddle-horses by Edward M. Curr (Melbourne, 1863), which deserves attentive study, the more especially that he writes entirely for Australians. The author is a native of Australia, who during twenty years had passed more time in the saddle than falls to the lot of most men. He describes his great experience in numerous countries, and had witnessed the performance and sufferings of the horse under almost every phase of labour, accident, and hardship, except the battlefield.

Mr. Curr unhesitatingly pronounces for the Arab, and denounces the system which has ruined the English horse; but as it is an Australian book on the same subject as that upon which I am writing, my readers can easily have recourse to it. But I must cite some of the statements which Mr.

Curr claims to have established and recapitulates, which are as follows :

'4th. The Arab or Eastern horse is a saddle-horse bred on sound axioms.

'5th. The Arab horse is a pure saddle-horse, and not a racer; his blood is pure.

'6th. No horse of any breed is so pure as the Arab.

'7th. The thoroughbred of England is almost entirely of Arab blood. So small has been his foreign admixture that, practically, his blood may be called Arab blood. . . .

'9th. Health, vigour of constitution, abstemiousness, stoutness, soundness, and longevity, are points in which the Arab horse is without a rival. He presents, as Youatt says, "the true combination of speed and bottom. . . ."

Mr. Curr says that he can find records of individual English horses having greatly distinguished themselves, but can find no instance of their having ever done so in a body, where they have been collected in bodies, as in the cavalry service, all testimonies seem to agree that their capabilities for work are much below those of Eastern horses, and that he can meet with no writer who has had personal experience of each who does not pronounce in favour of Eastern horses.

'14th. The saddle-horse of England is soft, unsound, and a failure.

'15th. Racing in England, so far from being the

means of improving the saddle-horse, has been his destruction. This fact is acknowledged and regretted by several English writers, who loudly claim Government interference on the subject.

'16th. The saddle-horse can never be brought to perfection until he be bred pure, as in the East.

'17th. The soundest, stoutest, and purest of horses is the Arab horse. He is a pure saddle-horse, unequalled in his performances and unrivalled in his desirability for this purpose.'

Mr. Curr asked how long would an English thoroughbred last in war, stand the bivouac, the wear and tear of cavalry practice before an enemy, with scarce or bad forage, cold, thirst, or hunger? 'A thousand times,' says he, 'rather give me the little Arab.' He wrote that our English cavalry horses were feeble; they measured high, but they did so from length of limb, which was weakness, not power. Also, how true a prophecy! How terribly he has been justified!

If Mr. Curr's words had been laid to heart by breeders in Australia, and his views had sooner had effect in England, certainly 50,000 to 100,000, probably 200,000, fewer horses would have been required in the Transvaal, and the lesser number would have done better work; certainly 5,000, probably 10,000, fewer of our countrymen would have succumbed to battle and sickness, and £50,000,000, probably £100,000,000, less money would have been spent, and the war been over at least twelve months sooner. But no: Mr. Curr and those who agreed with him were 'enthusiasts.' So the stable-boys, jockeys, trainers, and racers of sprinters, together with the 'bookies' and Captain Nolan's 'dandies,' were deemed better authorities; certainly they have proved to be the better business men, in so successfully indoctrinating the English world with their views, almost to the ruin of the Empire. And so it goes on still.

Gambling is the one important business, and gambling machines the things to breed! I think it will be admitted that I have not overestimated the number of horses that might possibly have been dispensed with, and the amount of money that might possibly have been saved, had it not been for the shocking deterioration I have referred to, when the numbers bought and the amount paid by the War-Office is taken into consideration.

According to the evidence given to the Royal Commission on the War, there were bought by the War-Office for the South African War 669,575 horses, mules and donkeys, of which 518,794 were horses and 150,781 mules and donkeys. Of these 400,446 were 'expended'—that is the word given in the evidence—during the campaign, besides those which were lost on the voyage to South Africa. The total expenditure on horses up to shipment, exclusive of freight, was £15,339,142.

Would not a continuance or much repetition of

such a sad state of affairs as that Commission brought to light be likely to cause the nation to invite a larger exercise of the prerogative than has been usual of late? A bad King checked by a powerful press could not have had matters worse; a good King governing would certainly have had them very much better.

As to the rejection of the opinions of men like those mentioned at the head of this chapter, and the rejection of the testimony of the ages concerning the supreme excellence of the Arab horse, which is scoffed at by 'sports' and jockey-boys, I take leave to cite a passage from Sir Edward Creasy's 'Fifteen Decisive Battles of the World': 'The truth of many a brilliant narrative . . . has of late years been triumphantly demonstrated, and the shallowness of the sceptical scoffs with which little minds have carped at the good minds of antiquity has been in many instances decisively exposed.' I would ask my reader which he would back—Job or the jockey-boy? For half-a-mile sprint with a light weight the odds would be in favour of the jockey-boy; but for a fifty or a hundred mile gallop in the desert, with a horse carrying 20 to 23 stone and the enemy behind him, there are few persons who would not back at very long odds the favourite of Job. In fact, the jockey-boy's mount would be dead before the Arab had got fairly into his second wind.

CHAPTER VII

SUNDRY ENCOMIUMS ON THE ARAB TAKEN AT RANDOM, AND INSTANCES OF THE LOVE OF THE ARAB BY GREAT SOLDIERS

BISHOP HEBER, in his 'Narrative of a Journey through the Upper Provinces of India,' says: 'My horse is a nice quiet, good-tempered little Arab, who is so fearless that he goes without starting close up to an elephant, and so gentle and so docile that he eats bread out of my hand, and has almost as much attachment and as coaxing ways as a dog.' My guests frequently notice the strange coaxing ways of my stallions, and my unbroken mares love to be petted, coming up around you for that purpose in the paddock. Although unbroken, and only handled when being weaned, they eat thistles out of the hands of the children of one of my men.

Captain Shakespeare, in his 'Wild Sport in India,' says that the Arab is the very best horse under the saddle that can be had in India for all general purposes.

Mr. H. Chichester Hart, in 'Scripture Natural History,' writes of the Syrian horses of to-day, that, no matter what the nature of the country, nothing comes amiss to them, and there is probably in the world no more sure-footed beast of burden to be found ; that they are docile and spirited and willing to the last extremity. Certainly these are Eastern horses, truly Arabs, though not the very best of Arabs, not being of the pure desert breed. They are often spoken of as Syrian Arabs.

Mr. Sydney Galvayne, in his article 'War-Horses, Present and Future,' says of Arab ponies that there was not a very large number of these valuable ponies sent from India to Africa, but what were sent made a great name for themselves and fully maintained their reputation for endurance and strength.

The Rev. E. J. Davis, in his 'Life in Asiatic Turkey,' writes that even hard work and starvation cannot tame his spirited little horse, which, in spite of being in bad condition owing to hard work and insufficient food, has never once stumbled, never been sick, and has borne the longest and most difficult marches with the utmost fire and spirit.

Mr. A. G. Hulme-Bearman, in his 'Twenty Years in the Near East,' refers again and again to the excellence of the Syrian pony upon which he crossed Lebanon, 8,000 feet, through snow up to the girths, then Anti-Lebanon, 6,000 feet, and after a few days' rest the pony took him back just as readily. A writer on the retreat from Moscow speaks of the Cossack pony (Eastern) as living on what it could get by scraping the snow with its feet, in pursuit 'indomitable, not to be fatigued, relentless.'

Mr. Adye writes that it was, of course, the Arab descent of the little animal so much in vogue in India which accounts for its excellence; and truly wonderful were the capabilities of the little hunters (some of them only 13.2) on which the redoubtable sportsman Major Shakespeare speared hog, bear, and even leopards, over broken and rocky ground intersected by nullahs and other obstacles, which render pig-sticking in certain parts of India the most difficult and exciting of all forms of hunting from the horseman's point of view. This corroborates what General Tweedie says, as above mentioned, in referring to which I have mentioned other instances of this wonderful capacity of turning and twisting, which alone could render such sport safe and possible. Mr. Ker, in his book 'On the Road to Khiva,' says that the Khirgiz, with Eastern horses, sit motionless on their saddles, aligned 'as if on parade.' Suddenly the foremost darts off at full gallop, and then, wheeling in mid-career, comes like a thunderbolt, all in one mad whirl of flight and pursuit.

'Bruni,' in the *Australasian* (September 6, 1902), testifies that the Indian records abound in proofs of the marvellous services rendered by the small horse, and notably by the Arab, and that on every hand the evidence was strongly in favour of the Arab and Arab cross for army purposes, and that of the value of the Arab cross we have had ample proof in Australia, because for endurance they had no equal.

Dean C. Worcester, of Michigan, U.S.A., writes of the Philippine ponies as having originated from the Andalusian horse or Barb, and, being well formed, sure-footed, and remarkably tough, making excellent saddle-horses.

Mr. George Flemming writes of the wonderful endurance of the Tartar pony; he gives one instance of the Russian courier, who used to ride from Pekin to Kiakta—500 miles—in twelve days, rest two days, and return in fifteen, and quotes a book by the Emperor Kienloong, published in Paris in 1770, translated by a Jesuit Father, alluding to those for racing as having a swiftness beyond comparison. These Tartar horses have been crossed again and again with Arabs.

Mr. Adye says that General Walker, Military Attaché to Berlin some years ago, when probably English cavalry were better mounted than now, was much exercised to account for the superior endurance of the Prussian troop-horses over the English. He was given as the chief reason the nearer affinity to pure Arab blood. He says that, when favouring the Arab, he was asked, Why go to the Arab when the English thoroughbred was a perfected Arab? To which he replied that the Arab was much hardier, that the thoroughbred was a more useful animal a hundred years ago than he is now, and he expressed his regret that the Arab was not properly appreciated in England; and then he prophetically added: 'Some day, perhaps in some future campaign, in which he happens to be brought into direct comparison with our present trooper, and is found to be going on for months after the latter is hopelessly done up or dead, we may have our eyes opened to his extraordinary merits.'

This was written before the Boer War. Alas that he should have been so accurate! To say that the English thoroughbred is a perfected Arab is nonsense, the jargon of the bookmakers; he is an Arab deteriorated—deteriorated by his being bred for sprinting, and spoiled by base blood.

In the *Leisure Hour* (May, 1902), W. J. Gordon, in 'The Horse-Supply of the World,' writes that in the Napoleonic wars the Russian horse (an Eastern horse), lived while the French horse died; that the only others that stood it were the little Arabs from the islands of the Levant. And he says that in the Austrian army much of the quality of their horses was due to careful breeding, especially in those from Hungary, which had a strong infusion of the Arab. And he shows the excellence of the Arab as a sire by the fact that the small Burmese tat, sturdy and sound, is, since the introduction of Arab stallions, developing into that useful but larger breed, the Indo-Burmese. And he adds that the riding-horses of Persia and Syria (allied races to the Arab, if not pure Arab, for the Arabs conquered all those countries) are better in quality than even the rough

RAFYK BEGGING FOR SUGAR.

customers like Burnaby's wonderful Arab, which he bought for £5.

Chambers's Journal (September, 1901, p. 609) says that the Connemara ponies are greatly indebted to the infusion of Arab blood, as also are the Orloff trotters and the Achil pony.

Mr. Wilfrid Blunt stated to his purchasers at his sale at Crabbet Park, in July, 1901, that the British Government had at last entered its name on the list of his customers, that the Scotch Breeding Commission had taken three of his best stallions to improve the ponies of the Western Highlands, and that the Government of India had decided on reorganizing its military studs, and true Arab stallions were to be used.

The *Register* (August 14, 1901) states that at this sale the Dutch Jockey Club of Java bought some Arab stallions.

Mr. C. B. Fisher states that he believes that the Arab and the Timor are the only two pure breeds there are. Where comes in the purity of the boasted thoroughbred if this belief of one of the most experienced and respected breeders of horses in Australia is well founded?

The *Australasian* (July 6, 1901) states that the breed of ponies which originally existed in Basutoland are supposed by the settlers to have been brought thither by Arabs from the northern regions of Africa, which is corroborated by a writer in the *South Australian Register* of June 10, 1901, on the

Boer ponies, who says that, 'as most of them are descendants of Arab stock, they are unrivalled for hard usage'; and 'Bruni' writes (September 6, 1903) that 'Boer ponies are said to be half-bred Arabs.'

These newspapers might have been more positive as to the Arab blood in these celebrated ponies, for Professor Wallace of Edinburgh, in his book on 'The Farming Industries of South Africa,' published 1896, after his official visit on the invitation of the Cape Government to report upon and advise as to those industries, shows that these wonderful South African horses are for the most part of Arab blood. He states that the first horses at the Cape were imported, soon after 1650, by the Dutch East India Company, and consisted of Arabs and Gulf Arabs. Note that he distinguishes between Arabs of the pure breed, like Mr. Wilfrid Blunt's, and the inferior breeds of the Gulf, such as are occasionally palmed off on India. Then he continues that, when inbreeding led to deterioration, the same company introduced Persian Arabs about 1688, that these became crossed with other stock, including Spanish horses (which, as I have shown, have a good sprinkling of Barb blood), and that recently the breed has been improved by crossing with Arab stallions.

On October 11, 1902, 'Bruni' writes: 'Since I wrote on the Arab as a sire, I have received several letters from horsemen in widely different parts of Australia, bearing testimony to the value of the

Arab as a sire calculated to improve the stamina of our horse stock. The most interesting of these letters is one received from Mr. R. R. Hogarth, a resident of the north-west coast of Tasmania. He gives the following instance of the powers of endurance of the high-grade Arab: "In December, 1900, my brother, weighing about 10 stone 7 pounds, rode a pony standing 12.2 hands from this place to Evandale Junction in one day. The distance is ninety-two miles. He left here at 4 a.m., and arrived at Evandale Junction at 8 p.m. He stayed an hour at Latrobe for breakfast, and another hour at Dunorlan for dinner, leaving the main-road a mile to call on Mr. W. Wyatt." To show that the pony was not injured by his long journey Mr. Hogarth rode him into Launceston and back—a distance of twenty-two miles—the next day. The road Mr. Hogarth describes as macadamized, and exceptionally hilly in parts. The pony was taken out of a grass paddock the day before he did the journey, having been running there for some time. The pony was by Dagobert, imported from New South Wales from a three-quarter-bred Arab mare by Maharajah, an Arab horse well known in the Evandale district. The feat performed by this pony far exceeds the European military race of seventy miles, in which no less than thirteen of the competitors were killed. Of the pony himself Mr. Hogarth says: "His walk and canter were perfect, while as to his trot—well, it was indescribable."'

An article in the *South Australian Register*, September 9, 1898, after quoting various favourable opinions, observes that in February, 1862, at Calcutta, the Arab Hermit, though defeated, gave Voltigeur's daughter such a stretching that the following day the mare had to be kept at home, and the Arab proved the winner. Their hardiness was such that many an Arab has continued year after year to add to his laurels in spite of a thickened suspensory ligament.

Mr. De Vere Hunt cites with approval an authority which asserts that none but a people long possessed of numerous and well-trained chargers could have planted the victorious banners of Islam on the Pyrenees as well as on the banks of the Ganges. He might have added—'and carried them to China.' He then sets out a letter from Lord Gifford, who was for twenty years a master of foxhounds, wherein the writer says that his little Arab was worth fifty of the gray, he rode him cub-hunting with Mr. Greaves, and he was active as a cat, and could put a leg anywhere. The horse was apparently not an Arab.

In the *South Australian Advertiser*, it was lately stated that the Arabian horse has been used in developing the military horses of all the European countries, and that the thoroughbred had deteriorated to a mere shadow, while the Arab had remained the same and was increasing in popularity in Great Britain.

'Cecil,' whom I have mentioned above, while

supporting Mr. Day in supposing that the Arab could not improve the racehorse—as a racehorse—admits that: 'For riding-horses, however, it is another affair.' For the army and the general public that is the whole question.

Major Arthur Griffiths, in an article in the *Fortnightly*, September, 1898, writes that another great merit in the Egyptian cavalry is their horse-flesh, sturdy little Syrian Arabs which have done an immense amount of hard work, and, although small for their loads, are so strong and full of spirit that they have never been sick or sorry all the year.

At the Battle of Omdurman the Egyptian cavalry, mostly Arabs and Arab crosses, were out all day on September 1 from daybreak on August 31, and not in till 3 p.m., and on September 2 they were heavily engaged with the Dervishes for several hours. They then advanced on Omdurman, and were sent in pursuit of the Khalifa; and the writer adds that it is really wonderful what the Arab pony will do.

The passage from Mr. G. W. Steevens' book above quoted as to the cavalry march to Omdurman shows the weight-carrying power of the Arab horse; for the 'little Syrian' is three-parts Arab—often, indeed, called Arab. This little horse with a light rider carried 18 stone on his back; with a heavy rider he carried 20 stone. I also cited the passage because it shows to demonstration the utter inferiority of the English horse, 'which had to be left behind at Cairo.' Mr. Steevens was only describing what he saw. He does not appear to have had any idea of lauding the Arab. It does not appear that he knew how nearly Arab the little Syrian is, nor does it appear that he had any idea of disparaging the English horse. He was describing a picturesque scene, and the reference to the English horse seems to have been quite an aside. 'Their own big, hungry chargers had to be left behind at Cairo!'

Dinah Sharp, in the *New York Times*, November 14, 1891, shows that the Arab has not deteriorated. She relates that Omar (who afterwards belonged to the late Empress of Austria, the finest horsewoman in Europe), travelled three days and nights over the hot and barren plains of the Arabian desert, with but 2 quarts of barley for food, and an occasional tuft of Sahara clover.

Miss Ella Sykes, in her recent work 'Through Persia on a Side-saddle,' writes that the horses they usually had were wiry little Arabs, about 14 hands high, plucky, enduring, and very easy to manage by their riders.

The Vienna correspondent of the *Mail*, recently wrote that the Hungarian horse had special qualities of endurance, which he attributed to his dash of the Arab blood, and that it was a great matter to have a certain strain of Arab blood in the troop-horse; for the Arab horse and the horse with the Arab blood will feed on indifferent forage which the English horse will not look at, and would retain condition when the latter was reduced to a bag of bones. The Hungarian horse had extremely hard bone, like the Arab, and consequently was seldom troubled with spavin, which was but too common among our own horses, whose bones are softer.

The *Windsor Magazine*, January, 1903, has it that the horses which are common to Hungary and Roumania are famous for their extraordinary strength, pluck, and sure-footedness. They both have a strong Arab dash.

In the 'Encyclopædia Britannica' art. 'Arabia,' it is said that trained European racers would easily distance a thoroughbred Arab on any ordinary course, but for perfection of form, symmetry of limbs, cleanness of muscle, beauty of appearance, for endurance of fatigue, for docility, and for speed maintained for distances so long as to appear incredible, the Nedjie horse acknowledges no equal.

Mr. Harold Leeney, M.R.C.V.S., in the *Live Stock Journal* Almanack for 1898, writing a scientific article on the castration of horses, showing its desirability, says that if exception—*i.e.*, non-castration—could be made to any particular breed, he would say that the Arab was the one with fewest objections as an entire. No other reference is made to the Arab in the article, and this incidental reference of course testifies in an unusual manner to his docility. It is said that if they have never been at the stud they are perfectly quiet; and I believe that they are not usually gelded in Egypt. I often show off the docility of the breed to my guests by mounting—I ought to say, at seventy-three, by climbing on to—my old sire, now twelve years old, in the paddock, without either saddle or bridle, and I have done this though close to him on the other side of the fence was another stallion. I have ridden him in great crowds and tents and shows and sports at Glenelg on Commemoration Day, and when he has got excited I have only had to speak to him to calm him down. This after several years at the stud.

Mr. W. G. Palgrave says that it is well known that in Arabia horses are much less frequently vicious or refractory than in Europe. Why, that is in the breed! Then he adds that this was the reason why geldings there were so rare. Miss Sara Linard, in her recent book on the horse, 1902, quotes a horse-parade described in the *Daily Graphic* of October, 1896, where four young ladies rode four Arab stallions, which, she says, before going to the stud are entirely safe, and which she also says is the case with Arabs only, 'who know how to behave themselves as gentlemen.' Many young ladies, visitors at my farm, from six or seven up, love to give my stallions sugar. But they are pure bred. They are 'gentlemen.'

I have read that the docility and the cleverness of the breed are such that, in Arabia, they lead the animal to bite and keep in the path those which stray. Now, it so happened that, when the grass began to spring, the horses, working bullocks, and cows, at Kingsford, where I used to be stock-keeping in the forties, used to wander—there were no paddocks—and it was my duty to go out in the morning and bring them home, sometimes a distance of three or four or more miles. There was always a tendency in cattle and horses under these circumstances to edge off from a man on foot, and so surely as any of the other horses, or any of the cows or bullocks, did this, my old stock-horse, half Arab, as I have said, was as prompt as a cattle-dog to rush out and bring them back by a nip. I often used to wonder how he acquired the habit. This was, of course, when he 'wasn't on' himself for a gallop. Occasionally some of those uncanny creatures which entered the Gadarene swine possessed him, and at such times he was the ringleader. That was when the 'old Adam' came out; but he would not ordinarily allow any of the others to lead or to depart from the right path.

In Dr. Liddon's 'Tour in Egypt and Palestine in 1886,' a description is given of a Bedouin Sheikh, a worthy descendant of Sir Walter Scott's Saladin. When he stuck his spear into the ground, his horse stood and watched him like a dog. When he returned after his rounds, his horse lay down and gave a low whinny, then the Sheikh lay down by his side, making a pillow of the horse, and they both slept, apparently, for half an hour. The Sheikh again went his rounds, and the horse, finding his master had no further intentions of going to bed, got up and stood by the spear all night. My groom often lies down between the legs of my stallions, which then walk round him inquiringly and caressingly, apparently pleased at his confidence.

Mr. R. Fitzroy Cote, a considerable author, in his 'Peruvians at Home,' says that at the Lima bull-fights all the horses permitted to enter the arena must be of pure Arab blood, and owing to their sagacity and the agility of their riders they seldom fail to escape the bull's horns. Mr. Cote was not writing up the Arab horse, and only mentions him incidentally; but doubtless the Peruvians had discovered his wonderful powers of twisting and turning, which have been illustrated in his boar-hunting in India.

The great traveller J. S. Buckingham, who at one time commanded a ship which made a long stay at each of the great marts of trade in the Persian Gulf, in giving an account of the trade there to India, and explaining the easy mode in which horses might thence be shipped, says that it was the usual thing for Arab horses to sleep standing, and to do so for years in succession, without ever lying down except when sick.

'Bruni' points out, on the authority of Mr. W. G. Hughes of Texas, that the foundation stock of the celebrated Mexican mustangs was the Moorish horses (Barbs) turned loose by Cortes. Desiring to breed from these mustangs, Mr. Hughes travelled over a large part of the United States, and finally found the horse he wanted in Nimrod, by a pure Arab sire, Vimr.

As showing the growing favour of the Arab, the racing gentlemen notwithstanding, the *Ladies' Field*, October 28, 1902, has an advertisement that 'a perfectly-shaped child's pony 11.3 hands, rising five, like a miniature Arab, jumps high,' was for sale. A racing man would probably laugh at this, but even supposing the man or woman who inserted this advertisement had been impressed by some drawing-room or fashionable novel, none the less does it show that the present general trend of opinion towards the Arab which 'Bruni' testifies to. It shows a belief that Arab blood is a recommendation, that there is a growing recognition of the excellence of the breed, a belief that it is the best that can be obtained in horse-flesh, and breeders who want to sell will be wise if they note it. If it be only a straw, it is the sort of straw which shows the way the wind is blowing. It demonstrates, in fact, that belief in the Arab is 'sinking in.' Can anyone wonder at it when he reads the facts collected in this little book?

'Faneargh,' in the *Sydney Mail*, writes that the old stock-horse of the overlanders of the early forties and fifties were largely bred from Arabs, that these old horses were of wonderful stamina, and their staying powers were marvellous.

The *Register*, September 7, 1901, reminds the public that the Arab horse stands cold as well as heat, and will eat anything that is given to him; that on half-rations or less his brave heart carries him through almost all imaginable difficulties; that it is difficult to overweight him, and he has always been more appreciated by foreigners than by Englishmen—of course because of sprinting.

Professor Watson writes that the African horses were smaller and shorter in the body than those bred in Australia, and, as most of them were descendants of the Arab stock, they are unrivalled for hard usage.

At Waterloo the Emperor Napoleon was mounted on Marengo, a beautiful little Arab, only 14.2 hands, and when wounded Napoleon mounted his white Arab mare Marie; and in another sketch of Napoleon it is stated that Marengo was brought by Napoleon from Egypt in 1799, and ridden by him at Marengo, Austerlitz, Jena, Wagram, in the Russian Campaign, and at Waterloo, and that his skeleton was still in the Royal United Service Institution.

The German Emperor at the army manœuvres in 1902 led the cavalry 'mounted on his Arab charger.' He may be a poet, but he is no dreamy simpleton. He is probably the hardest-headed man in Europe.

Lord Roberts at the Queen's Diamond Jubilee was mounted on ' his celebrated Arab.' Lord Roberts is not a drawing-room General, but, as stated by

Lieutenant-Colonel Maude in *Macmillan*, May 1, 1902, 'a perfect horsemen—one of the best in India—a man of the widest experience as to what horses can do in the field.' Colonel Maude states that General Roberts rode his Arab all through the Candahar forced march—'a type of the highest class of Arab.' By special permission of Queen Victoria, this horse, Voronel, wears an Afghan medal with four clasps, and the Cabul-Candahar star.

Abdur Rahman, late Amir of Afghanistan, writes in his autobiography (one of the most remarkable books of the day, 1900): 'At the end of our march both men and horses were well-nigh exhausted. I myself cooked some meat and distributed it among the men, who were almost fainting; the horses meantime lay down, unable to rise again. Only one horse, my own Arab, remained standing.'

Abdur Rahman was fighting for his life, and, like the Bedouin, had to rely on his horse for his preservation. The odds on the Cup and the Stud-Book were nothing to him. A racing sprinter would have been destruction to him. He wanted fact, not fancy; solid work, not delicate prettiness; and it can be hardly suggested that the German Emperor did not know a good horse. Why did they ride Arabs when the pick of the whole world was at their service?

In the autobiography of General Sir Harry Smith, of Aliwal, a very great soldier of wonderful energy, reference is frequently made to his celebrated Arab horse Aliwal, which carried the veteran in all the battles of the Gwalior and Sikh campaigns in 1847, accompanied him to the Cape, returned with him to England, afterwards served him faithfully in his commands at Davenport and Manchester, and was in his possession for eighteen years. It is related that on the anniversary of the Battle of Aliwal, when there was a full-dress dinner at the General's house, someone would propose Aliwal's health, and Sir Harry would order him to be sent for. The groom would lead him all round the dinner-table, glittering with plate, lights, uniforms, and brilliant dresses, and he would be quite quiet, only giving a snort now and again, though when his health had been drunk, and the groom had led him out, you could hear him on the gravel outside prancing and capering.

Sir Harry writes: 'I had one little Arab, not 14 hands, descended from Arabs; he never gave me a fall, and I never failed to bring the brush to his stable when I rode him; but with all the other horses I have had some awful falls, particularly after rain, when the sand is saturated with water and very heavy.'

It is further written of the General that he usually rode his little Arab Aliwal, and always when the troops were in line he would suddenly put his horse into a gallop and ride at the line, as if he were going to charge through them; that the men were, of course, well up to this trick, and stood perfectly steady, and the little Arab always suddenly halted within a foot of the line.

The following epitaph on his horse by Sir Harry, in his own handwriting, is still preserved :

'NEAR THIS STONE IS BURIED SIR HARRY SMITH'S CELEBRATED CHARGER OF THE PUREST BLOOD, ALIWAL.

'Sir Harry rode him in the Battles of Moodkee, Ferozesshahur, Aliwal, and Sobraon. He was the only horse of the General Staff that was not killed or wounded. He came from Arabia to Calcutta, thence to Lahore ; he was marched nearly over India, came by ship to England, thence to the Cape of Good Hope, and back to England. He was twenty-two years old, never sick during the eighteen years in Sir Harry's possession. As a charger he was incomparable, gallant, and docile ; as a friend he was affectionate and faithful.'

Is this all a romantic dream ? Can the opinion of a racing gentleman founded upon 'sprinting,' or of a stable youth founded upon 'tips,' or of a 'dandy' of Piccadilly, or of the 'best boy' of a Melbourne barmaid, be placed against the practical experience of all these great soldiers ?

In the Franco-Prussian War the Arab again proved his superiority. The *Times* of February 24, 1871, gave an account of the entry of General Bourbaki's army into Berne, and the distress of both men and horses, but it qualified this as to the Arabs by adding that 'undoubtedly the Arabs justify the established reputation of their breed for endurance by the very tolerable condition they presented and the comparative elasticity of their paces.'

Mr. W. G. Palgrave, in his 'Central and Eastern

Arabia,' vol. ii., says, of some horses then before him, that never had he seen or imagined so lovely a collection. Their stature was indeed somewhat low—he did not think that any came up to 15 hands; 14 appeared to be about their average—but they were so exquisitely well shaped that want of greater size seemed hardly, if at all, a defect. He says that they appeared a little, a very little, saddle-backed—just the curve which indicates springiness without weakness; every other part, too, had a perfection and a harmony unwitnessed, at least by his eye, anywhere else—an air and step that seemed to say, 'Look at me: am I not pretty?' Their appearance justified all reputation, all value, all poetry.

Captain Burnaby, in his 'Ride to Khiva,' says of horses of the Kirghiz, that no horses that he has ever seen are so hardy as these little animals. He bought one with saddle and bridle, 14 hands, for £5, of excessive leanness, and by his description only fit for the knackers, which in England would not have been considered able to carry his boots, yet, in spite of quite 20 stone on his back, he never showed the least sign of fatigue. There is Arab blood in these horses, or they are of a kindred breed. All over the steppes Arabic words are used, showing the influence of the Arabs in the past; indeed, they overran much of this country.

In July, 1270, a French expedition (the seventh Crusade), under Louis IX. attacked Tunis. Mr.

Pellissier, writing in 1844 on this Crusade, says that the Arabs attacked the French Crusaders every day, and that 'if one pursued them they fled; but when the French returned to their quarters, tired out by a bootless chase, the Arabs turned round and assailed their pursuers with arrows and javelins. This is exactly how they treat us to-day.'

In the latter sentence he referred to the Arabs under Abd-el-Kader in Algiers. It was as bootless a chase for the French cavalry to try to catch the Arab horses in Algiers in 1840 as it was for the same cavalry to try to catch the Arab horses in Tunis in 1270; 600 years had not lessened the difference in merit between the two breeds: the Arab was still *facile princeps*.

General De Wet could furnish instances yet sixty years later of other European cavalry having bootless chases after Arab horses. In 1535 the Emperor Charles V. attacked Tunis with success, and amongst the terms of the treaty of peace which was made it was provided that the suzerainty of Spain was to be recognised by a yearly present of twelve horses. No such term would have been made unless the horses had been known to have been of unusual excellence. You don't take coals to Newcastle nor Arab horses to Arabia. But you send them elsewhere. Another Bey of Tunis, Ahmed Bey, in 1842, sent, amongst other things, a present of an Arabian horse to Louis Philippe, King of the French. So that we have three Kings of France in three far-apart periods receiving presents of Arab horses from the Bey of Tunis, and there are scores of other instances where an Arab horse has been deemed worthy of being a present to be received by one Sovereign from another. Was I not justified in saying that it was childish of my unknown friend, above referred to, to say that there is neither speed, stamina, nor docility, in the Arab horse?

Napoleon Bonaparte, in his 'Observations on Egypt,' states that although discipline made 1,000 of the French cavalry superior to 1,500 Mamelukes, yet man for man the Mamelukes were the better —' two of them were able to make head against three Frenchmen,' because they were better armed and better mounted; and Sir Edward Creasy says that Napoleon is the best writer on the subject of Egypt that a general or statesman can consult.

The Mamelukes were probably Arabs, but were certainly mounted on Arab horses, and Cook's 'Guide to Egypt' cites Warburton as stating that the Mamelukes were the most superb cavalry in the world. Major Upton says in effect the same with regard to the present age: 'The real armour of the Bedaween horsemen, offensive and defensive, is the speed of his mare.'

Polybius wrote that it was the superiority of Hannibal's cavalry which gained him all his victories. That cavalry was Numidian—that is, Arab.

'Thormanby,' in a book on 'The Horse and his Rider,' whom I should by no means take to be an

Arab enthusiast, affirms that the Arab is in many respects entitled to take the lead among all breeds of horses; that his pace is rapid and graceful; that he is hardy, and can continue travelling at the rate of from fifty to sixty miles a day; that it is proved beyond doubt that for slow, continued work the Arab is immeasurably superior to his English brethren. That distance is the mileage that one of Mr. Quin's Arabs at Tarella, New South Wales, bought of me, went day after day during the great drought about the end of the nineteenth century, with, I believe, only native grass, or what was left of it. Is that properly to be called 'slow'?

'Thormanby' can, clearly, have meant 'slow' only as opposed to short sprinting with light weights; in fact, he admits as much in almost the very words that I heard applied to Mr. Quin's stallion, that an Arab seems at his own pace to be able to go for ever. But I deny that his pace is slow; it is very fast, as many a defeated army has discovered. 'Thormanby' describes two Arab horses sent to him from Bombay to Lucknow, which did not reach him for five months, having marched continuously, with many vicissitudes, continual forced marches, and irregularly and scantily fed, still arriving in perfect trim, and continuing to do fast work throughout the hot season. I note particularly the word 'fast,' which is the author's. 'Thormanby' might therefore have said more in the previous passage than to say the Arab was immeasurably superior for 'slow' continual work! He fairly enough says that, all things considered, he should prefer in the Indian or Egyptian climate an Arab to any other horse, habituated as he is from infancy to scanty food and water, and to enduring heat and rough usage, and above all with sounder legs and feet—a good-tempered, willing and docile slave, and a rare agent to traverse a distance in an open country. Another passage from 'Thormanby' shows how ill adapted the ordinary horsey man, used to the 'leggy, weedy creature who would fall over a straw,' is to judge of the merits of the Arab. Says 'Thormanby' of five Arabs of the ordinary stamp—by 'ordinary,' I take it, he means Bombay Arabs of the old style, not pure-breds of the desert—'To an eye accustomed to European horse-flesh they would have looked, perhaps, at the first glance like a lot of screws; but when you came to examine them closely, you found undeniable points about them, and a look of gameness that showed it was, at any rate, no plebeian animal that you had before you.' A former Duke of Newcastle, one of the best judges of horse-flesh then in England, shows how few people can judge an Arab accurately. He thought very little of the Godolphin Arabian!

'Thormanby' points out that the wild-horses of America, both North and South, have descended from Andalusians imported by the first settled Spanish settlers, and that they are fine animals, very hardy, and when caught soon docile. He describes the common amusement of the Mexicans and South Americans in charging like lightning, and stopping so suddenly that the horses' feet will exactly touch the wall, and even at times will tremble over a precipice, and yet wheel round in safety.

This is of a piece with the description given by Layard and many others of the Eastern Arabs, who would stop in full charge with their spears so close to his face that an accident would have caused his death. I have cited Major-General Tweedie's references to this, and those of several others.

'Thormanby' relates a story of Sir R. Gillespie on the Calcutta racecourse, when a tiger had escaped. A Bengal tiger is no kitten to play with. Sir Robert called for his Arab, a small gray, and attacked the tiger with a boar-spear, which was in the hands of one of the crowd. Immediately the tiger saw Sir Robert, he crouched for a spring, at which Sir Robert instantly put his horse in a leap over the tiger's back and thrust his spear through the animal's spine.

This grand and fearless little fellow was afterwards given as a present to the Prince Regent. Though he was like all his race, a born war-horse, cool in the presence of the tiger under a rider that he knew, and not afraid of jumping over him, yet, alas! he could probably not have won a half-mile race with 5 stone on his back! How sadly degenerate! Nevertheless, he was not quite 'so extinct as the dodo' on that occasion!

Mr. W. K. Kelly, the traveller, in his book on 'Syria,' 1844, says that the Bedouin and his horse should be seen together. When the rider's feet are on the ground, he creeps listlessly about, and the horse stands tamely, looking hungrily after the few blades of grass. But when the Bedouin springs into the saddle an electric energy seems breathed into the man and horse. The horse makes the air whistle with his speed, while his streaming tail often lashes his rider's back.

This is exactly what Madam Ida Pfeiffer writes in her 'Travels in the Holy Land,' about fifty years ago. She said that at first sight they looked anything but handsome. They were thin, and generally walked at a slow pace, with their heads hanging down. But when skilful riders mounted them they appeared as if transformed. Lifting their small, graceful heads with fiery eyes, they threw out their slender feet with matchless swiftness, and bounded away over stock and stone, with a step so light, and yet so secure that accidents very rarely occurred. It was quite a treat to see them.

Madam Pfeiffer and Mr. Kelly both dwell on the Arab's powers of endurance. Mr. Kelly says they are most remarkable. His on more than one occasion carried him for sixteen or eighteen hours at a stretch without food, and once he cantered him from Hebron to Jaffa, nearly fifty miles, without pulling bit. At the end of such a journey, Arab horses, he says, get only a few handfuls of barley, no bedding or grooming, and generally the saddle is not removed. They are sure-footed and exceedingly sagacious, and exhibit a wonderful degree of activity and fleetness. Then he cites Baron von Taubenheim, first equerry to the King of Wurtemberg, who, writing to a friend, reminded him what an Anglomaniac he (the Baron) was, but said that nevertheless from henceforth he should set the Arab horse above every other, from experience of his extraordinary performances. The Baron describes the horrible roads of Lebanon —rocks over which the horse has often to mount or descend two or three at a step, loose rolling stones, a track running jaggedly and unevenly along the verge of a precipice. Yet along such roads as these the Arab goes on without flagging from six in the morning till eight at night, and he averred that he never discovered the least flagging, even in the last quarter of an hour, and for many days he literally never took hold of the reins.

The Rev. Dr. Porter, in his 'Five Years in Damascus,' refers to these dreadful roads of Lebanon, which, he says, 'are startling when your steed assumes a vertical attitude or passes along a precipice brink, where a false step would hurl him hundreds of feet below.'

After many other instances of endurance, cleverness, bottom, and docility, Baron Taubenheim says that he knows that vanity would make him in his own country again seek out a six-foot-high English horse, but that he also knows that the Arab is capable of doing much better service. For the day of battle he should, perhaps, make choice of an English hunter, but for a whole campaign, says he, 'give me one Arab in preference to two English horses.'

He also says that a traveller feels amazement to think that in such a country men can trust themselves upon horses where you would expect to see them mounted only on goats. Those horses don't fall over a straw. The Baron's vanity which he speaks of gives you a part of the key to the Anglomania vanity, the desire of being on a tall horse—the vanity of the horsey youth in top-boots and knee-breeches, whom the *Times* satirizes as a 'ten-dollar amateur'; the vanity of the Piccadilly masher prancing before the dames in the Park; the arrogant vanity of the insular mind, which thinks that nothing can be good which is not English. The other part of the key to this absurd Anglomania is the gambling.

In another place Mr. Kelly says that it is only in the East that you can form a just idea of the Arab horse, and he devotes a full page to enlarging on his merits, his beauty, his gentleness, his picturesque form, his caressing manner to his groom, his playfulness, his inquisitive attention, evincing as much certainty, force of character, and varied play of feature, as the emotions of mind on the face of a child. Many of my guests have noticed and spoken of this caressing manner shown by my young horses, as also their inquisitive attention and wonderful appearance of intelligence. It has been stated that an Arab would prefer his horse to be stolen rather than injured in a long and heavy chase, and that he has been known to rejoice, by reason of his pride in her, when his favourite mare has carried the thief safely away from his pursuit. If he is to be kicked, he hopes that it will be by a horse of pure breed!

Dr. Porter writes of the arrival of a stranger who drew up after a very rapid pace, whose mare stood patient and gentle without symptom of weariness or quickness of breathing, but with expanded nostril and proud eye. 'I could see,' said Dr. Porter, 'why the Arab loves his horse.'

Mr. Frederick Drew, in his book 'The Northern Frontier of India,' says that Baltistan is one of the homes of polo, which is so ancient a game that it was played in Constantinople in the middle of the twelfth century. 'The ponies of the Baltis,' he says, 'may be taken fairly enough to embody the experience of generations of players as to the right kind of animal. They stand about 12.3 or 13 hands, rather large-boned for their size, of compact make, broad chest, deep shoulder, well-formed barrel, well-ribbed-up, good hind-quarters, and a small, well-shaped head. This well describes a small Arab; anyhow, the creature to which Mr. Drew refers is an Eastern horse, and certainly more or less crossed with the Arab.

Mr. W. P. Hogg, an American gentleman, in his book 'The Land of the Arabian Nights,' after several casual and cursory remarks as to 'handsome Arab horses,' 'a mettled Arab,' 'a beautiful full-blood Arab horse,' and their ' wonderful endurance,' and so on, describes his inspection of the stables of the Pasha at Babylon, where there were a score of the finest Arab horses, and naïvely says that, although he is not especially a horse-fancier, he would fully appreciate the present were the Pasha to give him one of those beautiful animals, so intelligent, docile, and graceful in every motion. Everybody seems to notice their beauty.

The Hon. F. Walpole, in his book ' The Ansayrii,' writes of an Arab mare he was shown of the Anazeh : ' She was worthy of the pen of a Warburton or a Lamartine : clean gray, with black mane and tail, silvered at the end ; her skin thin as a kid glove, and the long hair as fine as that which drops over the shoulders of beauty. The eye was bright, wild, and flashing ; the nostrils full, almost bell-shaped ; tall and strong, yet light and active, she well deserved her name—The Beautiful.'

In 'Modern Persia,' C. J. Wills, M.D., describes a fourteen-hand pure-bred Arab which he bought, with a huge scar of a spear-wound a foot long on his shoulder, otherwise perfect, of angelic temper, but small by the side of the Persian horses, as all pure Arabs are ; his muzzle almost touched his chest as he arched his neck, and his action was very high yet easy; he seemed an aristocrat; his thin and fine mane and tail were like silk.

He says that he had that Arab ten years; he never was sick, and he never had to strike or spur him; a pressure of the knee and a shake of the rein would make him do his utmost. And he was a fast horse. 'Small as he was, he carried my 12 stone comfortably, and as a ladies' horse he was perfect, having a beautiful mouth, while he followed like a dog, and nothing startled him or made him shy.'

He speaks, too, of the Arabs which come from Bagdad as all that the heart can desire, except as to size, being seldom more than 14.2. Which is the better—14.2 that can carry one, or 16.2 that cannot?

The *Australasian*, April 2, 1904, in showing that the success of mule-breeding largely depends on the sire, says that the best mules in America are by Jacks descended from Catalonian sires imported from Spain—introduced to Spain centuries ago by the Moors, and always carefully bred. Who can doubt that this excellence is owing to the Arab stock owned by the Moors, which made the Andalusian jennet celebrated? Who can doubt after this the prepotency of the Arab sire, and his ability to benefit any breed he mates with, when even his hybrids became famous? Mr. Sydney Galvayne also testifies to this excellence of the American mule.

Captain R. V. Davidson, formerly of the Indian Staff Corps, writing of boar-hunting in India in the *Wide World Magazine,* says that 'he and Bethune Temple were on Arabs, and could count on their turn if it came to jinking,' and that when again and again 'the active brute, scenting danger, jinked away to right or left, his stanch little Arab followed him like a cat.'

Mr. F. C. Webb, M.I.C.E., in his 'Up the Tigris to Bagdad,' relates that they took on board three splendid Arab horses, which he would not have written if the Arab is only what some of the racing gentlemen affirm. An observation like this—by the way, as it were—is almost better testimony than a designed panegyric.

Professor A. B. Davidson gives a very celebrated line by Imrulquars, an ancient Arabian poet, describing the skirmishing of the horse and the irresistible impetus of his charge :

'Attacking, fleeing, advancing, backing at once,
Like a block of rock swept down by the torrent from a height.'

He gives part of another poem, in which is the line :
'My heart is with the horsemen of Yemen.'

The reader asks why I cite this. Because I am not writing for the 'knowing ones,' and I desire to show beyond all cavil that, at all times, in all countries, amongst all peoples, the Arab horse was famous. Such fame could never have been achieved for a breed that did not deserve it.

M. Tisset, in relating his travels in 'Unknown

Hungary,' says that all along the Turkish frontier, and especially in the upper military borderland, a small race of horses of Barbary origin is found well suited to those rugged and rocky countries, which corroborates the statements that the Hungarian horses are largely indebted for their excellence to Arab blood.

Count Henry Krasinski, a Polish soldier, in the 'History of the Cossacks of the Ukraine,' says that their horses are small in make, but extremely vigorous, and proof to all kinds of fatigue, clear all difficulties of the ground, carry their riders everywhere with facility, and are, like their masters, content with the most meagre fare ; and he describes them as hovering round the enemy like a vapoury cloud, augmenting, fading away, or dissipating entirely again, to form into shape when required. This fortifies the accounts I have given of the Arabs of Tunis in the third Crusade, and of the Arabs of Algiers recently in the time of General Daumas.

These Ukraine horses are Eastern, and, if not pure Arabs, have been improved by Arabs, and are of a kindred race. Count Krasinski states that at the great annual fair in the government of Volhynia 100,000 horses are often to be seen from all parts of Russia, Poland, Austria, and Turkey, and even Persia. The Kurdish mountains as well as Asia Minor were celebrated for their breed of horses in the time of the prophet Ezekiel (xxvii. 14).

In Mr. E. H. Parker's 'Thousand Years of the

Tartars' it is stated that Tukuhum of Koko-nor, one of their rulers, who reigned in the sixth century, obtained a number of splendid Persian mares for breeding purposes, and their young obtained great repute for swiftness. Of course, these were 'Eastern horses,' and yet not up to the level of the pure desert-bred Arab.

Mr. W. B. Harris, in his 'Journey through Yemen,' states that the Arabian King Tubba-el-Akran took an expedition to Samarcand, and afterwards, in A.D. 206, Abou Kariba, another Arabian King, invaded Chaldea, and defeated the Tartars of Adubijan, so that all this country from Arabia to China was saturated with the blood of Arabian horses.

I see by the London *Daily Telegraph*, February 6, 1904, that the Sultan of Morocco sent a present of six pure Arabs to President Rooseveldt from Fez, one for the President himself, the others for his wife and children, the one for himself being a pure white thoroughbred. In ancient times white horses were most esteemed; *e.g.*, Herodotus says that the Sicilians paid an annual tribute of 360 white horses, Arabs or Arab crosses, to Darius, King of Persia. Sicilian horses, of course, came from Africa (Barbary, etc.), just opposite. Other instances are given of the preference for white horses; Arab horses have always been deemed worthy of being gifts from royalty to royalty. Incidentally several instances appear in this little work. I may summarize a few more which I have come across in casual reading:

In the year 800 Haroun al Raschid sent a present of five Arabs to Charlemagne. In the tenth century the Grand Vizier presented to the Caliph fifteen Arab horses of the best breed.

In 1131 Alexander I. presented an Arabian horse to the Church of St. Andrews. Mehemmed Khan, Governor of Balk, presented Shah Abbas, amongst other presents, with fifty horses of Turkestan. The Imaum of Muscat sent a present to King William IV. of some horses of the purest breed of Arabia.

Megder, a Tartar Prince, one of the great conquerors of history, sent a present of Tartar horses to the Chinese Emperor about 200 B.C. In A.D. 635 the Turkish Khan sent a present of horses to the founder of the Tang Dynasty in China.

When Ibn Batula visited Sarunda in Asiatic Turkey in 1332, the Sultan presented him with a dress of honour and riding-horses. They never thought of sending pigs or oxen or Suffolk punches, admirable in their way as these creatures may be, and all these horses were Arab horses or Eastern horses more or less improved by Arabian blood.

The favourite horse of William the Conqueror was of Arab breed.

Richard Cœur de Lion so admired the Arab that he brought two Eastern horses from Cyprus, and Edward III. purchased fifty Spanish steeds (of course Barbs), and got special permission for their safe transport through France and Spain.

Edward III. was a great warrior. Did he not know the value of the creature he purchased?

Major Butler in his 'Great Lone Land,' describes a wonderful little horse of the prairies whose endurance could not be excelled day by day. He feared that he must give out; but not a bit of it! he still held gamely on, seldom travelling less than fifty miles a day, nothing to eat but the grass, and no time to eat but the frosty night. These prairie horses were descended from Spanish importations—Andalusians, *i.e.*, Arabs or Barbs.

Count Rziewuski (Russian) says that Asiatic horses are of one family, different from the European horses, except the English, which have much Arab blood, and that Napoleon did his best to improve the horses in France, but they were *far inferior* to English horses. This was in the middle of last century. The Count could not say that now. The Count also stated that the Poles had spared no expense in introducing Arab stallions, and gives many instances. Why were the English horses of that day superior to the French? Plainly, because up to that time the English had used the Arab very much more than the French, as the Stud-Book shows and as Count Rziewuski states. Why are they inferior now? Because they have fallen off from the use of the Arab.

M. Chateaubriand, in his 'Travels in Greece,' testifies to the hardihood of the Arab horse, and

MISS DE BEAUGY (BY RAFYK OUT OF A HEAVY CART-MARE).

enters at length into what hardships he can stand, and says that a horse of well-known noble blood 'will fetch any price,' while you can get an ordinary horse for 80 or 100 piastres.

Major Denham, on losing a fine Arabian, describes how keenly he felt the loss, and says that although he was ashamed of it, yet he was some days before he could get over it; the animal had been his support and comfort through many a dreary day and night. Almost all riders of Arabs have felt the same sort of affection. As several authorities have observed, 'the Arab is always a gentleman.'

Captain Thomas Brown, 1830, says in his book that the Turkomans trace all their best horses to Arabian sires. They believe that the race degenerates unless 'refreshed,' and they are therefore most anxious to obtain fine Arabian horses. They live upon plunder, and march from 70 to 105 miles a day for twelve to fifteen days together without a halt. They have been known to go 900 miles in eleven successive days. Yet a sprinter would run away from them for a sprint—but for a sprint only. Where would be the sprinter at the end of the fifteen days of 100 miles a day?

The use of the Arab by the Turkoman is further alluded to by Mr. Henry Norman, M.P., in his book on 'All the Russias,' fifty years after Captain Brown wrote. He says that the Cossacks on the Armenian frontier are supplied with rifles by the Government; their wiry little horses are their own.

Russia has imposed peace on the Turkoman, so, in spite of Imperial Commissions and the importation of Arab stallions, the fleet and tireless Turkoman horse, with his flashing eye and scarlet nostril, is extinct for ever. Alas that it should be so! All honour to Mr. Wilfrid Blunt for his keeping the pure breed alive!

Captain Brown says that the horses of Turkey are principally descended from those of Arabia, Persia, and Barbary, have great fire and spirit, are extremely active, and he cites Mr. Evelyn as describing one sent to England as a perfect beauty, spirited, proud, nimble, turning with swiftness, in a small compass, and then quotes great authority as saying that nothing can surpass the Arab's gentleness, and that his obedience to his master and groom are very great.

Captain Brown also says that in the Mysore country the Princes and people of rank have a superior breed sprung from Arabian blood, and that the Mahratta country has also long been celebrated for its horses, which have much of the Arabian blood in them.

He refers to the East India Company as keeping very fine stallions, generally of the English blood. He says that the produce of these are good parade horses, with more show than the Arabians, but they were unable to stand the same fatigue, nor had they the same mettle. This is corroborated by the *Australasian*, March 2, 1904, fifty-four years afterwards, which states that at the great Durbar at Delhi there was a ten days' polo meeting, that the English ponies first gave in, the Australian lasted a day or two longer, but the only ones who stayed throughout the match were the Arabs! Yet they have neither staying power, courage, nor docility! *O tempora, O mores!*

And Captain Brown sums up by saying that of late too little attention has been paid to the introduction of foreign Arab or Eastern stallions, asks where can we find such horses at the present day, either as racers or stallions, as Eclipse, Childers, King Herod, Matchem, and others; and attributes the present failure to the departure of our present racers from the foreign blood—in other words, that since racing men have abandoned the use of the Arab their horse is failing.

Sir Samuel Baker, in his ' Tributaries of the Nile ' writes : ' Never was there a more perfect picture of a wild Arab horseman than Jali on his mare. Hardly was he in the saddle than away flew the mare, whilst her rider, in delight, threw himself almost under her belly while at full speed, picking up stones from the ground. Never were there more complete centaurs than these Hamran Arabs : horse and man appeared to be one animal, of the most elastic nature, that could twist and turn with the suppleness of a snake.'

Further, in speaking of a particular horse Aggahr, in hunting a lion, who flew along as easily as a cat, he says that Aggahr's gallop was perfection, and his long easy stride as easy to himself as to his rider; there was no necessity to guide him, he followed an animal like a greyhound, and sailed between the stems of the trees, carefully avoiding the trunks, so as to give room for the rider.

'And once a Hamran,' so Sir Samuel relates, 'who was hunted by a rhinoceros who unexpectedly charged, clasped his horse round the neck, and, ducking his head, blindly trusting to Providence and his good horse, over big rocks, fallen trees, thick thorns, and grass 10 feet high, with the infuriated animal in full chase only a few feet behind him, the horse doubling like a hare.' That is nearly as bold and as manly and as dangerous a sport as to run 800 yards on a smooth level sward for a ladies' purse, with silks and satins fluttering along the lawn!

Sir Samuel also describes a lion-hunt, where his horse Tetel stared fixedly at the lion and snorted; but Sir Samuel patted and coaxed him, and he did not stop his advance till his rider checked him, when within about 6 yards from the lion, the horse facing the lion with astounding courage, both keeping their eyes fixed on each other, the one beaming with rage, the other with cool determination. Sir Samuel then dropped the reins on his horse's neck—a signal which Tetel perfectly understood—and he stood as firm as a rock, for he knew his rider was about to fire. Tetel never flinched, Sir Samuel fired, and the lion dropped dead. But what is that compared to the noble achievement of a jockey in winning a town plate?

Yet one more incident from Sir Samuel's book: 'Roder Sheriff, on a bay mare, facing an old bull elephant waiting a good chance to charge, slowly and coolly advanced till within about 8 yards of the elephant's head, who never moved; the mare snorted, gazing intently at the elephant, watching for his attack. Sir Samuel for an instant saw the white of the elephant's eye, and called out, "Look out, Roder—he's coming!" as, with a shrill scream, the elephant dashed upon the mare and her rider like an avalanche.' Roder Sheriff had never won a Derby, so, of course, you suppose the benighted man was killed! Not so, however. In Sir Samuel's words, 'Round went the mare as on a pivot, and away over rocks and stones, flying like a gazelle.' For a moment Sir Samuel thought that all must be lost; but he describes how Roder watched the elephant over his shoulder, and lured him on till the horsemen behind came up and hamstrung him. Yet of such mares we are gravely told that they have neither speed, stamina, nor docility!

Caulincourt, Duke of Vicenza, when Ambassador to Russia in 1807, saw a review of the Horse Guards raised by Paul I., the finest corps of horse in Russia, and reported that their Arabian horses 'were of immense value.'

In the 'Souvenirs of Military Life in Algeria,' by the Comte De Castellane, he says of a hawking-party that 'the Arab horsemen were mounted on the fleet mares held in unbounded estimation.' Of one mare he says : ' Her action was so light that she might, according to the Arab phrase, have galloped on a woman's bosom.' Of course, a jockey or a racing trainer would sneer at this, naturally : he is *so* wise in horses—'one of the knowing ones.' Yet I think that the opinion of a French officer, often dependent on his horse for his life, engaged in war, with as brave warriors as there are in the world facing him, might be fairly considered to be rather more valuable than that of men engaged only in sprinting races, as to which horse is the better for the ordinary purposes of humanity.

Mr. George Flemming, in 'Travels in Mantchu Tartary,' says that the Russian courier used to ride one pony 500 miles to Pekin in twelve days, rest a day, and return in fifteen, on the most unfavourable sort of forage. He relates that their own rides had been long and without intermission, and their ponies looked none the worse, though they were eight or ten hours in the saddle daily, doing forty or forty-five miles a day, and travelling nigh 700 miles of rough country, nothing less than that average on miserable fare—bran and chopped straw.

Whether Tartar or Turkoman or Mantchu, all those ponies have been indebted to the Arab cross.

Mr. John Hill, in the *Live Stock Journal* Almanack, 1903, writes that he was much impressed by the foals and young stock of, amongst others, the Arab

Mootrub, and, again, that it is surer by far to breed up from the beautiful little Exmoor mare with the Mootrub cross on top. Further, that two very beautiful youngsters were shown from Exmoor dams and an Arab sire. He speaks of a beautiful little pony as a typical Arab in miniature, a clear proof of the Eastern ancestry of the Welsh mountain pony. In 'The Breeders' Directory' and in the advertisements of the same book are several announcements as to Arab sires.

Mr. Winwood Reade says that Cyrene, in Northern Africa, was 'famous for its Barbs, which won more than one prize in the chariot-races of the Grecian games.' Further on he says that the Berbers of the Carthaginian army were a splendid Cossack cavalry.

I give in Appendix II. the testimony of several large horse-breeders in the interior of Australia to the excellence, docility, and endurance of Arab stock got by pure stallions.

Sir Edward Creasy, in his 'History of the Ottoman Turks,' relates that when Mahomet II. heard in 1451 of the death of his father, Amurath II., 'he instantly sprang on an Arab horse and galloped off towards the shore of the Hellespont.' And he says that the Sultan Amurath, when making in 1638 a triumphal entry into Constantinople, 'rode a Nogai charger, and was followed by seven led Arab horses with jewelled caparisons.' Nogai is between the Caspian and the Black Sea, in the country of the Kirghiz, whose horses were partly Arab.

The first of these extracts from Sir Edward shows the reliance placed by the successful Sultan on the Arab horse at a great crisis, for often, if not mostly, many of the candidates were massacred straight away by some rival claimant. The second extract proves the admiration shown for him, and the honour always done him by a great conquering race, who conquered by the endurance, the speed, and the docility of their horses.

General Sir Thomas Edward Gordon, Military Attaché at Teheran, says that the Persian horses are small, but very wiry and enduring, capable of very long journeys. On one occasion, owing to some great man having got the post-horses ahead of him, he was driven to continue the use of those he had been using for ninety-six miles right away, with only three hours' rest at one place and one hour's rest at another.

He was shown the Royal Stud racehorses, Arabs from Arabia, and riding horses, deer-like Arabs of the best blood.

According to Madame Waddington, wife of the French Ambassador, the Russian Emperor Alexander III. always rode his little gray Cossack horse. He rode it at his coronation, and some days afterwards at a review.

Lieutenant-Colonel Prejevalsky, a Russian, says the Mongol riders go at full speed across the desert like the wind, and their horses possess wonderful powers of endurance on very indifferent feed; they will live where other horses would perish. The great traveller, Captain Wood (J.N.), says the same.

Colonel Ramsay says that the Parsees give immense prices for high-caste Arabs, and that Sir Jamsetjee Jeejeebhoy has superb English carriage-horses, but they cannot stand work in the Bombay climate. That is what Mr. Carwardine, a well-known Australian stock-owner, tells me of the Kimberley climate in North-Western Australia—that only Arabs can stand work there. Colonel Ramsay also describes the funeral of a grandee of Spain at Valencia, where 'there were some splendid turn-outs — Arabs of the purest breed.' And he speaks of his own regiment, the 14th Light Dragoons, as 'splendidly mounted on Gulf Arabs.'

Colonel Durand describes a horse he had in India as perfectly untiring, having sinews of steel, a bold, intelligent eye, and feet of flint—he never rode his equal on a hillside—and he goes into ecstasies over his other wonderful qualities, with his 'easy wolf's canter, eating up mile after mile without a check, a present fit for a king.' He says that none but the Arab could show such a combination of courage, fire, endurance, and general temper. His bold heart was the only one he trusted in implicitly.

Mrs. Frances Macnab, in her 'Travels in Morocco,' writes that she could not say that she ever met with a horse in Morocco which had any faults or ill-temper to be compared with other horses, and they would walk all day without food. In her own horse there was not a scrap of vice in his whole nature.

Mrs. G. R. Durand, wife of the British Minister to the Shah of Persia, in her book writes that the Bakhtiari horses are often beyond price, of pure Arab race, as hardy as beautiful; quite extraordinary in the way they carry their riders over rocks and stones—they scarcely ever make a mistake, and their legs seem to be as hard as steel. A little black mare 'carried her rider as if she had wings.' Mrs. Durand herself had a little gray Arab, who used to come into her dining-room and stroll round the table, pushing his head over their shoulders and whinnying gently for bits of bread. At a Simla dinner-party he came round the table just like a big dog.

Mr. J. H. Sanders shows that tradition had always affirmed that the Percheron, the most active and beautiful of all heavy breeds, is indebted to the Arab for his good qualities, and that recent research in France proves it. What the Darley Arabian was to the thoroughbred, that, says Mr. Sanders, was the gray Arabian Gallipoli to the Percheron. The American Percheron Stud-Book attributes the starting-point of the breed to the overthrow of the Arabs by Charles Martel at the Battle of Tours in the year 732, which left the fine Arab and Barb steeds of the defeated Arabs in the hands of the victors. It also shows that that infusion of Arab blood was strengthened by the finest of Arabian stallions brought back by the Crusaders, and was kept up at irregular intervals by many French nobles down to 1820. The form and other distinctive marks of the Arab, says Mr. Sanders, were thus stamped upon the Percheron.

The Arab breed, he says, was also the foundation of the celebrated breed of Orloff trotters established by Count Orloff, who imported a gray stallion named Smetauxa, from Arabia, to whom a Danish mare was bred, from the progeny of which cross the breed was founded.

And the now equally celebrated breed of American Morgan trotters is also mostly indebted to the Arab blood for its excellence, through Grand Bashaw, a Barb imported into America from Tripoli. In fact, says Mr. J. H. Sanders, this Oriental blood, wherever introduced, in all nations and all climates, has been a powerful factor in effecting improvement in the equine race. Yet, says Mr. Day, for practical purposes this same noble creature is as extinct as the dodo. *O tempora, O mores!*

Marco Polo noticed the superb qualities of the Arab in A.D. 1260. He says that excellent horses were bred in Yemen and taken to India, and numbers of Arab chargers were despatched from Aden to India, and 'fine horses of great price' were sent to India from Persia. Colonel Yule has a footnote that these latter horses were probably the same class of 'Gulf Arabs' that are now sent, which, as the 'Encyclopædia Britannica' says, are not equal to the pure Arabian.

Old Marco also speaks of the great excellence of the horses of Turcomania and Badakshan, remarkable for their speed, which go at a great pace even down steep descents, where other horses neither would nor could do the like, which subsist entirely on the grass, and are very docile. And he describes how the Turkomans pretend to run away in battle, turn in the saddle and shoot, the horses doubling hither and thither, just like a dog, in a way that is quite astonishing.

He also mentions several instances of the marvellous endurance of these Eastern horses. One accomplished 900 miles in eleven days, and another went from Teheran to Tabriz, returned, and went again to Tabriz, within twelve days, including two days' rest, a total of 1,100 miles. And he tells us that the Tartars, from converse with the Assyrians, Persians, and Chaldeans, acquired their manners and adopted their religion. He should have included the Arabs, for the religion was certainly theirs; and he might also have added that the Tartars acquired many of the Arab horses. In truth, I rather think that it was the Arabs, and not the Assyrians, Persians, or Chaldeans, that Marco ought to have referred to.

And Laurence Oliphant says that these Turcoman and Badakshan people attained to some degree of civilization by reason of their commercial relations with the Arabs, and that his experience proved that their ponies possessed great pluck and powers of endurance.

Long before Marco Polo's time far Eastern Asia was on the watch for Arab horses. Knei Shan (probably Khojend towards Merv) was 'celebrated for its horses of divine race.'

China went to war with the Great Wan in 104-103, and again in 109-98 B.C., for the possession of this country and its horses, which were undoubtedly Eastern horses—most probably Persian Gulf Arabs.

In 'The History of Russia' (Bohn's Library) the success of the Tartars is attributed partly to their 'being masters of the provinces which produced the finest horses.'

Mr. Shaw, in his 'Visits to High Tartary,' frequently refers to the handsome horses. He describes a sport where a dead goat is thrown on the ground, and the horsemen try to pick it up without leaving the saddle; when one succeeds he is chased by the others, doubling and turning, their hands seldom on the reins, banks and ditches jumped while they are half out of the saddle, galloping with one another, trusting entirely to their steeds when tugging with both hands at the goat. But, says he, 'the Toorkee horses seldom make a mistake.'

The Rev. Dr. Henry Lansdell (1893) writes of his travels in Central Asia, that, fearing his horse would slip, he dismounted, but found that was for the worse, since the horse proved the surer footed, and he had to remount and trust to the animal.

Sir Henry Layard describes clouds of Bakhtizari and Arab horsemen in mimic fight, pursuing each other, bringing up their horses on their haunches at full speed, firing guns as they turned in their saddles, and performing various feats.

Sir Henry was once chased, and his horses were weary, having been nearly twenty-four hours without rest; but, says he, 'they were sturdy beasts, and eluded their pursuers—it was wonderful!' The horses were able to bear great fatigue, and required little nourishment. Could Carbine have saved him?

He describes Mehemet Taki Khan's magnificent and beautiful Arab mare of pure blood, and the exercises of his horses of the finest Arab breeds—galloping to and fro, wheeling in narrowing circles, while their riders discharged their guns from behind, picked up objects at full speed, or clung at full length to one side of their horse, in order not to offer a mark to the enemy, and so on. How would these exercises suit your thoroughbreds, or your cavalry horses which ran into the streets at Winchester, and into the sea at Southampton?

Mr. Selah Merrill, of the American Exploration Society, writing of his journeys in Syria and Palestine, says that on one occasion he was ten hours and forty minutes in the saddle, and that on another occasion he was seventeen hours in the saddle one day, and fifteen hours the next; that the horses had a remarkable faculty of finding the way, and that, when riding in a difficult place, if you trusted entirely to your horse, you were almost certain to pass it in safety.

The Rev. Hugh Price Hughes, describing his journey to Jordan and the Dead Sea, writes (1901) that his chief dragoman was 'magnificently mounted,' as also were the four Arabs who were his escort. They put their splendid Arab horses through pretty and skilful performances.

A recent special correspondent writes in the *Land of Arabia—Ararat*, that the region was celebrated for its breed of horses, high-spirited, well bred, and noted for great endurance.

Disraeli writes in one of his letters: 'Hunted the other day, and was the best man in the field, riding an Arabian mare.' They rode much more cruelly in those days.

CHAPTER VIII

HORSES OF ANCIENT ARABIA

I TRUST I may be permitted here somewhat to digress in consequence of a matter which I noticed after I had written most of this book, viz., a passage in an Australian newspaper which stated that down to the Christian era the Arabs had no horses, a statement which has been used to detract from the purity and merits of the Arab breed.

Say some people : 'Oh! if there were no horses in Arabia before Christ, the old story about the pure Arab is a myth.' Of course, that is a non-sequitur.

I am not concerned to investigate this statement very deeply, as it does not seriously affect the practical question, because a breed kept pure since the time of Christ—say nearly 2,000 years—may be fairly enough called a truly pure breed; yet as the statement opens up one of the most fascinating subjects that could possibly be inquired into—the history and literature of the early peoples of the Bible—a subject which has always had for me the very deepest interest from my youth up, owing to early lessons and associations, I may be permitted a few words on the subject. I am not disposed offhand to accept the statement, and, indeed, I doubt it. I feel it the more necessary to allude to it because in its support it has been suggested that the Arabs had no horses even at the time of Mahomet, who it is also said had no horses; and so it is contended that the whole of the story about the Arab horse is a myth, the dream of some stupid poets. Indeed, many people believe this. It is strange what some people will believe!

I may be the more excused for doubting the statements referred to because there is by no means unanimity of opinion amongst the students of such questions, and all has not yet been learned of the truth of the subject.

Discoveries are being made daily which upset our yesterday's knowledge, and rival professors alternately differ and agree. It has been said of Professor Stubbs, for example:

> 'Where from alternate tubs
> Stubbs butters Freeman,
> Freeman butters Stubbs;'

and by Professor Stubbs:

> 'Froude informs the Scottish youth
> That parsons have no care for truth,
> While Canon Kingsley loudly cries
> That history is a pack of lies.'

Which is like the dispute of a century ago as to musicians:

> 'Some declare that Buonocini
> Compared to Handel is a ninny:
> Others say that to him Handel
> Is not fit to hold a candle.'

Therefore I may be excused for stating my own opinion, derived largely from early reading on Biblical history, which has not yet been finally upset by later learning.

Probably the 'higher criticism' has had its influence in leading to the statements which I doubt, but, according to Professor Sayce, the higher criticism is nothing but 'the baseless fabric of subjective imagination,' and he says that research is constantly demonstrating how dangerous it is to question the veracity of tradition.

Dealing with the question as to Mahomet first, of course he had no horses in his early life. He was poor, and had no means to buy horses. He often had to hide from his enemies, and finally to fly his country. But after he became successful he had horses. That is so well known that there is no necessity to enlarge on it.

The other assertion, that there were no horses in Arabia before Christ, is a wider and more interesting matter, and also more difficult; and although I am not prepared to dogmatize or to pretend to affirm positively to the contrary, yet I think I shall show some good grounds for believing that there really were horses in Arabia before Christ.

Why should not the Arabs have had horses before Christ?

The Arabs and the Hebrews were of near kindred, alike descendants of Abraham, and lived close together. Scores of the names of places and men, and of the incidents in the Old Testament, refer more or less to Arabia and the Arabs.

Abraham has been called an Arabian Sheikh—in fact, Disraeli so spoke of him—and Moses has been said to have been an Arabian and a king of men amongst the Arabian races. Edom, Nebaioth, Sheba, Hazarmareth, were in Arabia or parts of Arabia, and possibly Ophir. If Ophir were not in Arabia, it was probably part of Africa peopled by Arabians. In the time of St. Paul Damascus belonged to the kingdom of Northern Arabia. The Ishmaelites were Arabs, or more or less Arabs. So I think were the Midianites, the Amalekites, and many other of the tribes or nations mentioned in Scripture.

Disraeli wrote of the children of Israel as an Arabian tribe, and said that the Arabs were only Jews upon horseback, which, however, would be a displeasing sentiment to Sidi Mohammed in Morocco, who recently told a French author that the Arab horse was too noble an animal to bear so despicable a burden as a Jew.

The Hon. Lieutenant Walpole's book entitled 'The Ansaryrii and the Assassins' gives from the Book of Jasher, mentioned in Scripture, an account (legendary of course) of the birth and youth of the patriarch Abraham, whom Nimrod had ordered to be destroyed, and of a dialogue between Terah, Abraham's father, and the King, in which the father begged for his son's life:

'Terah said: "Ayou, the son of Mored, offers me gold and silver if I will give him the horse of great price your majesty gave your servant."

'And Nimrod answered: "Art thou a fool, to give thy horse for silver or for gold? Of what worth will it be unto thee when thou hast no horse?"

'"Live for ever, O King!" said Terah. "Of what use will silver and gold be unto me when I have no son?"

Here we find in hoary antiquity an Arab chieftain having a horse, and comparing it in value with the life of a son.

The Hebrews had horses. They had been sufficiently harassed by Pharaoh's chariots in the exodus to learn their value. The Egyptians pursued them with both chariots and horsemen: 'the waters returned and covered the chariots and horsemen' (Exod. xiv. 28). Josephus says there were 600 chariots and 50,000 horsemen. I read Josephus when I was twelve years old, but of course I know that much has been discovered since he wrote.

The Jews had learned to value horses so much that they were forbidden (Deut. xvii. 17, 18) to go down to Egypt to get horses. The early prophets complained that the horse was regarded by politicians more than the God of Israel Himself.

Yet although forbidden by Jehovah, Solomon (1 Kings iv. 26) had 40,000 stalls of horses for his chariots, and 12,000 horsemen. That was 1,000 years before Christ.

In 1 Kings x. 45 we read that all the earth sought Solomon, and 'they brought every man his presents . . . horses and mules.' Does not all the earth include Arabia? It certainly does. To the evangelical that would be sufficient. But I think it is clear, not only that it does in the general meaning of the words, but that the text intends that meaning.

Why should the Arabs have valued horses less than the Jews? There was every reason why the Arabs should have valued them more, and, valuing them more, should have procured them even if they had not got them, although I maintain that they had. They were more necessary for the national existence of the Arabs than of the Jews.

About Jerusalem and in much of Palestine horses could not be advantageously used, whereas in Arabia they were a necessity. If the Jews, who could do without horses, possessed them, is it likely that the Arabs, a kindred and adjacent people, who could not well, if at all, do without them, should not possess them also?

With the huge traffic that was carried on between Egypt, Syria, Judea, Babylonia, Assyria, Mesopotamia, and various localities in Arabia, and the intermarriages and near relationship between the Arabs and the Hebrews, it seems to me hard to believe that the Arabs had not horses many hundreds of years before Christ.

Among the Kings to whom the Lord God of Israel told Jeremiah to take the winecup of His wrath, and to drink and be mad, were 'all the Kings of Arabia' (Jer. ii. 24).

St. Paul visited Arabia (Gal. i. 17), and St. Peter heard the Arabians 'speak in their own tongue' (Acts ii. 11).

Ezekiel writes of the noise of the horsemen and of the wheels of the chariots, and also (xxiii. 7-15) of the Assyrian captains and rulers, all of them desirable young men 'riding upon horses.' Not horses driven in harness only. Isaiah (chapter xxx.) writes: 'We will flee on horses'; chapter xxii. 6: 'Elam bare the quiver with chariots of men and horsemen.'

The prophet Habakkuk writes (i. 8): 'Their horses also are swifter than the leopards, and are more fierce than the evening wolves: and their horsemen shall spread themselves, and their horsemen shall come from far; they shall fly as the eagle that hasteth to eat.'

In addition to these general references to the horse, besides very many more, we learn that the Arabians were engaged at times in fighting against, and at other times in fighting for, the Hebrews in battles where there must have been horses.

The Arabians were joined with the Philistines in harrying Jehoram, King of Judah, and they overran his country and carried away all the substance that was found in his house, not to mention his wives and his sons (2 Chron. xxi. 16, 17). This allied army could not have operated without horses.

In 2 Chron. xxviii. 16 we learn that the King of Judah sent to the Assyrians to help him; and the Rev. Professor Sayce says that the Assyrians conquered Edom and the Queen of the Arabs, who had overrun Judah, as the Chronicles mention.

Edom was Northern Arabia. Also, according to Professor Sayce, Herodotus was told in Egypt that that country had been attacked by Sennacherib, the King of the Arabians and Assyrians—an alliance which, it is impossible to doubt, also must have had horses.

It is recorded that the first Babylonian dynasty of Urukh lasted 458 years, and then there followed nine Arabian Kings, who ruled in Chaldea 245 years. The King of Egypt overran Judah with 60,000 horsemen (2 Chron. xii. 3).

The Assyrians had horses galore, and if the Arabians helped them, and if nine of the Arabian Kings ruled in Assyria, I venture to think that the Arabians must have had horses also.

As showing the close intimacy between the Arabians and the Hebrews, I read that there is an ancient Hebrew sepulchral tablet in the British Museum, brought from Aden, which is in the ancient Hebrew characters, and that, while the characters of the inscriptions on Mount Sinai are mostly Hebrew, the language they utter is the old Arabic. This shows how very close was the connection; in fact, it has been said that the Arabian thread runs through the long lines of earth's history almost since the Flood; and it has also been said that the Arabic language is of primeval antiquity, and prior to all of the other Semitic tongues.

The Assyrians were allied in blood and language to the Arabs, and they were frequently fighting one another. Sennacherib, King of Assyria, in a translation given by Professor Sayce of a despatch of his, says that Hezekiah of Judah sent to him ' the Arabs whom he had brought for the defence of Jerusalem.' And the Professor also says that Sennacherib's son Esar-haddon sent an expedition 'into the heart of Northern Arabia,' and that his son Assur-bani-pal chastised the ' tribes of Northern Arabia,' but that afterwards Babylonia, Egypt, Palestine, and Arabia, made common cause, and delivered Egypt from the Assyrian yoke. The Professor also gives an inscription of Sargon, King of Assyria, which states that he slaughtered certain ' distant Arab tribes,' which he enumerates.

Job was Arab, as were also his three friends. He was an Arab Sheikh who lived on the edge of the desert and thoroughly knew the desert and its ways, and the marvellous poem is saturated with Arabian lore. There is not a single reference in it to Hebrew law or to the sacred writings; and although it now appears in the Hebrew language, and is the most splendid creation of Hebrew poetry extant, it is said that it was originally written in Arabic, and was afterwards translated into Hebrew. I speak as I have learned, and am no Hebraist. Job was a descendant of Ishmael, and was not a Jew. He lived some 600 years before Solomon, over 2,000 years before Mahomet. He knew the horse, and evidently loved him as much as General Harry Smith of Aliwal or Field-Marshal Roberts loved him—perhaps even more. Job's description of the horse (xxxix. 19-25) has never been equalled either in prose or poetry, and no description of anything that was ever written by the hand of man is more magnificent.

In these days of non-Bible-reading in schools, I may be excused for giving it. The college boy and the 'Girton girl' may set it off against the jargon of the racing stable. It will do them no harm. It will not even harm a jockey-boy. I the more readily quote it because a leading man in this State, a good judge of horses, very recently confessed to me that he had never read it. I myself have read it many times, and I have never read it but it has made my blood run hotter:

'Hast Thou given the horse strength? hast Thou clothed his neck with thunder?

'Canst Thou make him afraid as a grasshopper? the glory of his nostrils is terrible.

'He paweth in the valley, and rejoiceth in his strength: he goeth on to meet the armed men.

'He mocketh at fear, and is not affrighted; neither turneth he back from the sword.

'The quiver rattleth against him, the glittering spear and the shield.

'He swalloweth the ground with fierceness and rage: neither believeth he that it is the sound of the trumpet.

'He saith among the trumpets, Ha, ha; and he smelleth the battle afar off, the thunder of the captains, and the shouting.'

That description was not written of Mr. Day's 'heavy-shouldered, slack-loined, little-legged brutes that would fall over a straw.' It was written of the Arab, and the Arab only; and the same chapter of Job that I have quoted, in verse 16, shows, on the testimony of an Arabian, that horses were, at all events, then ridden; for he says 'the ostrich scorneth the horse and his rider.' This was 1,500 years before Christ.

A good many people think of the Arabs as only a few scattered tribes of Bedouins roaming about with their tents and their horses, themselves only semi-savages and thieves. No doubt some of them are. There are such even in England. But they were a great people with a great literature. It has even been supposed that the ancient Egyptians were indebted to the Arabs for their civilization, and Professor Sayce has stated that he believes inscriptions may be discovered to show that Southern Arabia was in a high state of civilization 5,000 years before Christ.

We Europeans are indebted to them for our numerals and our algebra, and we got Euclid through the medium of the Arabic language.

They built the Alhambra, which has been termed the 'Queen of all Architecture.'

From the very earliest age they sent out colonies to Asia, Africa, and even Europe. Their language is one of the richest in the world. It was the language of science and philosophy for centuries when Europe was barbarian, and the race is a fighting race second in power and bravery to none of the sons of men.

Mr. Steevens, in his book 'With Kitchener to Khartoum,' writes of the Dervishes at Omdurman (largely of Arab blood): 'The honour of the fight must still go with the men who died. Our men were perfect, but the Dervishes were superb—beyond perfection.' In fact, according to this, the Dervishes, man for man, were as superior to our men as Napoleon said those other African Arabs, the Mamelukes, man for man, were superior to the French horsemen; and the horses of the Dervishes as superior to our weeds — for those had to be left behind at Cairo—as Napoleon confessed the Arab horses of the Mamelukes were superior to those of the French cavalry.

The poetry of the Arabs is superior to most, and has never been excelled by any. Their country was never thoroughly conquered. They defied the Persians and the Assyrians; neither Alexander the Great nor the Romans could subdue them. In the seventh century they sent out armies which attacked and conquered one-half of the then known world; defeated the Greek Emperor Heraclius at Damascus; overwhelmed a Persian army with great slaughter, and mastered Persia; conquered and occupied Egypt, Syria, and Spain; at the Crusades they drove united Europe back from Jerusalem. To this very day they largely defy the Turks, who never thoroughly conquered more than a fringe of their country, and they even worry the English around Aden.

Physically and mentally they yield to few races, if any, of mankind, and intellectually they surpass most. We owe to them the revival of learning and philosophy in Western Europe, and widespread as was the empire of the Arab sword, it has been less extended and less durable than the empire of the Arab mind.

It has been said that Terence was a Moor, and that it is certain that Juba was of unmixed Arab blood.

A large measure of the success in war of this great people they owed to their horses. What could they have done with Flanders mares or 'big hungry' and 'weedy' thoroughbreds?

The Hyksos, or Shepherd Kings, who invaded and conquered Egypt about 2,000 years before Christ, had horses. They were Arabs, or partly Arabs, and their portraits on the tombs and temples, apart from history, prove that they were so, and show the distinguishing dress and the distinguishing features of Arabs of the present day. The 'Encyclopædia Britannica' says that it was these Hyksos who introduced horses into Egypt. They could not have introduced horses into Egypt unless they had them.

Mr. Winwood Reade, in his before-mentioned book, written after two years' travel in Africa, expressly studied the question, and after consulting a mass of authorities, says that the Hyksos were Bedouins of the Arabian Peninsula, and that their conquest of Egypt was owing to the fright of the Egyptians at their horses, for the Egyptians had never seen a horse before. And he calls them Arabs. The Egyptians uprose, and 'the Arabs were driven back.'

The Rev. W. J. Dean, in 'Abraham and his Times,' says that the word 'Hyksos' means Bedouins, and that they were of Semitic origin from Canaan and Arabia; and one of, I believe, the most recent authorities, Professor Reinisch, says that the original stock of the Abyssinians came from the Sabeans from South Africa, and Lady Anne Blunt maintains that, according to the Sabean traditions, they first settled in Egypt, and were the Egyptians who oppressed the Jews. Mr. Dean says that Abraham appeared in the land in the time of the Hyksos. Mr. Winwood Reade says—and Mr. S. Laing, in his 'Human Origins,' says almost the same—that the Hyksos were a shepherd people, settled in Canaan and Yemen, who crossed over into Africa. In Barbary and Sahara they were called Berbers; in the Valley of the Nile, Egyptians; in the desert and Yemen, Arabians; in Palestine, Canaanites; in Mesopotamia, Assyrians; in the lower course of the Euphrates, Chaldeans or Babylonians.

Gibbon, in the 'Decline and Fall,' says that Arabia is the genuine and original country of the horse; and he also says that the merits of the Barb, the Spanish, and the English breed are derived from Arabian blood. Concerning this latter statement there is no doubt whatever.

A very learned writer in *Knowledge* (August, 1904), however, differs with Gibbon's former statement, and adds that horses were not depicted on Egyptian frescoes till 1900 B.C. But he says that the whole shape and make of the horse then depicted was decidedly of the Arab type, which tends to support Gibbon, for that was about the time of the Hyksos. If their horses were not Arabs, how account for the whole shape and make of the horses depicted on the frescoes being of that type?

A note to Gibbon states that at the end of

the thirteenth century the horses of the Nejd were esteemed sure-footed, those of the Yemen strong and serviceable, those of Hejaz most noble (all Arabian); and that the horses of Europe were generally despised as having too much body and too little spirit. This contempt is certainly justified by the article in *Knowledge*, which shows that the Western horse arose from the 'hog-maned breed,' a totally different stock from the Arab. Whether Gibbon be entirely right or not, the article in *Knowledge* demonstrates the characteristic purity of the Arab for nearly forty centuries.

But there is more positive proof—if anything can be proved in respect of these ancient monarchies. In 'Stones Crying Out' reference is made to a rare tract by Schultens, 'Monumenta Historia Arabie,' which refers to engraved marbles, near Aden. On reference to these marbles it was found that there were mentioned 'two most wonderful ancient poems,' discovered by Abderrahman, Viceroy of Yemen, so long ago as 660-670—' discovered' over 1,200 years ago. Schultens had taken his information from an earlier writer, and the Arabs of the seventh century ascribed the poems to their heroic age, which may be possibly about the time of Job, very possibly earlier. One of the lines of one of these most ancient poems runs: 'Proud champions of our families and our wives, fighting valiantly upon coursers with long necks dun-coloured, iron gray, and bright bay.'

That does not look as if before the time of Christ there were no horses in Arabia, nor as if they were not ridden.

But whether the Arabs had horses before Christ or not is really not material. The horse of which I am writing, now called Arabian, is the Eastern horse, in medieval literature as I have before said, frequently spoken of by that description, and sometimes called Barb. The Godolphin Arabian and the Godolphin Barb were two names for the same horse. Yet, by whatever name you call him, his breed was known thousands of years ago—at least 7,000 years ago, I believe.

You find pictures of him thousands of years before Christ, harnessed in chariots, which, by the way, is no proof that he was not ridden. There is a splendid picture of three abreast in a chariot in Professor Sayce's 'Races of the Old Testament' (1893), with heads and forms as beautiful as can be found to-day in the purest Arabian. The author of 'Stones Crying Out' says that the Assyrian sculptures show that 'their horses were of noble blood, perhaps Arabian,' and are drawn from the finest models. I maintain that those horses certainly were Arabian—that is, that they were of the same grand breed which is now called Arabian. There is a drawing of the head of one in a picture of Sennacherib in his chariot, which is a perfect likeness of the handsomest Arab you could find to-day.

SIR JAMES P. BOUCAUT ON FAROUN, BY MESSAOUD (SOLD TO RUSSIAN GOVERNMENT).

I venture, therefore, respectfully to think that the authorities I have quoted in this chapter tend to show alike the antiquity and the purity of the breed, and that it is the breed now and always heretofore used and valued in Arabia.

We know how he is valued in Arabia even to the present day. We know how he was valued 3,000 years ago, when Job wrote, and when the early Hebrew prophets complained that he was more valued than the God of Israel. In the intermediate time, early in our era, the pure breed was valued quite as much, for we read that Abu-Obeidah, Commander-in-Chief of Omar, who was the second Caliph, after the Battle of Yermouk, which overthrew the Roman power and decided the fate of Syria, awarded a double portion of spoil 'to those who had true Arabian horses.' Even thus early, A.D. 623, the pure Arabian was distinguished and specialized, and was valued beyond other breeds in all Eastern countries.

An impure breed could never have maintained its essential sameness and characteristics so uniformly for so many thousands of years as the Arab has done, nor would men of all nations have so uniformly and so universally praised an animal which was not of surpassing excellence. If he pass away by human folly, then, as General Tweedie says, you will never see his like again.

When I think of the history and the triumphs and the intellectual grandeur of the Arabs, I know not whether I feel more grieved or angry that my countrymen have paid greater heed to the gambling requirements of bookmakers, jockeys, and stable-boys, almost to the ruin of the nation, than to the precepts, the learning, the wisdom, and the experience, of forty centuries of so great a people.

CHAPTER IX

MR. DAY AND THE DODO

BEFORE citing authorities to show the sort of horse which it will pay to breed in Australia, and probably in England, I take the liberty of making an observation or two on the criticism of Mr. W. Day with regard to the Arab, who says that 'for practical purposes he might be as defunct as the dodo.' Of course, by practical purposes he must mean breeding for racing and by racing, sprinting. He cannot mean for the brewers' drays, for the spavined thousand-pounders would not do for such use as that, neither would Persimmon. But if, as Mr. Day admits in another place, the cross with the Arab was an extremely fortunate one, and achieved a great and happy result at the time—note the words, 'a great and happy result'—it seems very absurd for him to say that the Arab for practical purposes might be as defunct as the dodo, even with the limited meaning I have mentioned. If the Arab achieved in the past such a success, then in saying that he might be as defunct as the dodo Mr. Day takes upon himself to affirm more than it is possible for any man rightly to affirm, unless he have scientifically tried the experiment, which he never seems to have done.

Besides, the statement that the cross with the Arab achieved a great and happy result at the time is somewhat apt to mislead. It seems to assume that there was some English breed apart from the Arab, which only needed a little Arab improvement, whereas, as I have shown, the English thoroughbred is greatly Arab, spoiled by cross-breeding with inferior English and Flemish horses.

Mr. Day's utterances in the face of authority, even in the face of his own admissions, appear to be founded on the prejudice of a racing man in favour of the breed which produces ' long-legged, pampered weeds,' for he himself says that out of thirty-six picked stallions, supposed to be the best of the sort in England, no less than fourteen (perhaps more) were not fit for the purpose. Note ' picked stallions,' and compare this with the statement in the Australian Stud-Book that many stallions in that list are not worthy of entry.

I think a neutral mind would rise from the perusal of Mr. Day's book impressed with the sure conviction that it was the English thoroughbred that for practical purposes (except for a half-mile sprint with a light weight) was defunct like the dodo, 'and only to be reinvigorated by large crossing with the foundation stock of his breed—*i.e.*, the pure Arab.'

The inevitable bias of a gentleman in Mr. Day's

calling is pointed out by Sir Walter Gilbey:
'The man who has devoted himself exclusively to
the production of one class of horse cannot rid himself of the prejudices he has necessarily formed; he
cannot put aside his bias in favour of a horse suitable
for sport.' It is natural.

A great number of the authorities to which I refer
show that Mr. Day is wrong in making such a
comparison with the dodo, and that the Arab, if
wisely used, would greatly benefit the thoroughbred
in everything that makes the horse valuable, save
only with regard to half-mile sprints, and it is by
no means certain that he would not improve the
racer even for that.

It would be impossible to accept the accuracy of
Mr. Day's assertion about the dodo, even for sprint
racing, without trial and scientific selection for
three or four or more crossings, which has not
been attempted, because no desire has been shown
to accept such a course, for the breeder has been
too utterly impatient. He wants to gamble with
his two-year-old, and cannot afford delay. This
is notorious.

There is more reason in the Bedouin, who will
not have his pure breed spoiled by the impure
English thoroughbred at any price. He is a better
judge of horse-flesh than a sprinting trainer—*i.e.*, of
horse-flesh for use, and not of horse-flesh for
gambling. The Bedouin's life depends upon his
horse—not merely for one or two short gallops, but

for long and heavy gallops, often repeated during many years, with heavy weights, for which purpose he wants a horse with staying powers, with a hardy, docile nature, and with courage, that can go long journeys day after day on bad feed, with but little water, and that can be relied on. The Bedouin knows the thoroughbred cannot do this, and that his own horse can, and he knows also that the cross will spoil his own breed, so he will have none of it.

As Major-General Tweedie, in his great work, writes: 'Nothing would induce the breeders of the pure Arabian horse to use the English stallion. . . . Experience has fortified them against the idea that mixed and impure blood would improve the pure and superior.'

The Bedouin has experience of a different nature from that of the racing breeder. The experience which refers to the dodo is that of the racing breeder—experience with regard to a half-mile sprint with light weights: just a few half-miles in the course of the creature's life, pampered, doctored, forced, and then useless. The experience of the Bedouin is experience with regard to forced marches, long gallops, heavy weights, short rations, frequent battles and the saving of men's lives during many years.

Supposing that Socialistic principles were to be hereafter carried out to their extremest extent, and that the State ultimately undertook the supervision of the breeding of the human animal—as to a certain extent prevailed in ancient Sparta, and as to a certain extent has been suggested of late years by some Socialist cranks in Europe—can it be imagined that the inspectors of breeding of that good time to come would seek to invigorate the blood of the Norman house of 'Vere de Vere' by crossing it with a good fat, lusty mulatto? Hardly! Why not? The answer would be, Because you could never be sure that the black blood would not come out. Like breeds like, and there is always a tendency to revert. The Bedouin knows this, and will not run the risk of having his horses ruined by 'Flemish fat.' They can rely upon the one; no man can rely upon the other.

Mr. J. L. Lupton writes that the Eastern horse has maintained his type through a thousand years. He might have written through many thousand years.

In an account in the *Times* or the *Mail*, April 13, 1904, of some instructive preparations illustrating the evolution of the horse and the origin of the thoroughbred, at the British Museum of Natural History at South Kensington, the writer, when referring to the pit in the skull found in some Indian fossil horses, states that, from the fact that a similar pit is found in the skulls of Bend Or and of Stockwell, it seems highly probable that the Arab stock which forms the foundation of our thoroughbreds was originally imported from India.

The writer of this paragraph, and the scientists who investigated the fossils and the skulls, were not thinking of Mr. Day or of Bedouins, but have, nevertheless, given strong support to the practical wisdom of the Bedouins in determining to keep their breed pure, and not to have it soiled by the impure blood, always existent, if frequently latent, in the English thoroughbred.

It was after writing the above observations on Mr. Day's reference to the dodo that I was favoured by Mr. C. B. Fisher with the perusal of Captain Upton's book, ' Newmarket and Arabia : An Examination of the Descent of Racers and Coursers.' He was a Captain (afterwards a Major) in the 9th Royal Lancers, and therefore presumably knew something about a horse, and in all probability knew better than Mr. Day, as to what sort of animal to breed for military and general purposes. He asks pertinently enough, as to an argument such as Mr. Day's dodo absurdity, whether it had never struck breeders that the natural speed of the pure Arabian might have been increased to even a greater degree than that now exhibited by his half-bred descendant, if Arabian blood had been bred from alone for a few generations? Whether it had been proved that Arabians have not as high a rate of speed? Whether we have procured young stock, and by careful training ascertained their capabilities? And then he asserts that until all this, and more, has been tried, no one can say that the Arabian is inferior in speed, and that to say so is an unfounded assertion. Then he gives a long list of races of Arabs in India, showing many of them most remarkable speed, with defeats of many English horses, and endurance that the latter cannot approach. One Arabian, Gray Leg, 14 hands $1\frac{3}{4}$ inches, was never out of training for seven years, from 1861 to 1868, ran eighty times, and won fifty-one races at all distances and under all weights. Two Arabs, Crab and Oranmore, met for the Bengal Cup heats, two miles, in 1845; they had previously run three or four well-contested races, winning alternately. For the Bengal Cup they ran five heats, the first won by Oranmore, second a dead heat, third won by Crab, fourth a dead heat, fifth won by Crab, with 8 stone 7 pounds each. Next month they met again, and ran a dead heat; Oranmore won the deciding heat by a head. Surely, says Captain Upton, this is something like the stuff of which racehorses should be made!

Then, in answer to the argument put forth in order to excuse the frequent defeat of English thorough-breds by Arabs, that only second- or third-rate racers have found their way to India, he asks : 'Will any man be bold enough to say that the best Arabians have ever appeared on an Indian racecourse, either?' On this, I observe that many authorities think that it is a rare thing to get a pure Arab from Bombay. Then Captain Upton shows that the Arab's per-formances on the Indian turf prove him to be the better horse, because even when vanquished he has come out the next day, and day after day, and won, whereas the victors have been unable to put in an appearance. Captain Upton gives the times and weight, of which I mention a few:

1847, Baron, half-mile, 8 stone 7 pounds, fifty-four seconds.

1844, Sir Hugh, half-mile, fifty-one seconds.

1847, Child of the Islands, three-quarters of a mile, 8 stone 7 pounds, one minute twenty-one seconds; Minuet, one mile, 8 stone 3 pounds, one minute fifty seconds; Child of the Islands, one and a half miles, 7 stone 8 pounds, two minutes forty-eight seconds.

1848, Honeysuckle, 14 hands 1 inch, two miles, 8 stone, three minutes forty-eight seconds; Honeysuckle, two miles, 8 stone 11 pounds, three minutes fifty seconds.

1846, Selim, three miles, 9 stone 5 pounds, five minutes fifty-four seconds.

Captain Upton asserts that even when beaten the Arab has proved his superiority as a horse, and supports his views as to what might be done by breeding and training pure Arabs for racing by the opinion of Mr. Blenkiron, of the Middle Park stud, who agreed with the Captain, and said that he would have tried it if it had been brought to his notice when he first commenced breeding.

The truth is that breeders cannot afford to honestly try the experiment. The delay would be too great for Crœsus, at 500 and 600 guineas for service to one mare, and in all cases too great for ordinary breeders, because, in order to pay the ordinary breeding, stable, and training expenses, horses have to be run as two-year olds.

But even conceding that Mr. Day has formed a correct judgment with regard to the effect of the Arab on short-distance racehorses, his opinion can have no possible relation to the question of general breeding for use, and especially on the question of breeding for army remounts, and is calculated to do infinite mischief.

CHAPTER X

WHAT SORT OF HORSE TO BREED

THERE are three classes of authorities which I shall now cite as to the sort of horse which ought to be bred: First, those who specially prefer and name Arabs, which is the most numerous and an increasing class; secondly, those (and these are fewer) who, without mentioning Arabs, describe the sort of horse that is wanted, and whose descriptions are only completely answered by Arabs; and, thirdly, those who warn you what not to breed, and whose warnings apply to just the sort of horse which the Arab is not. Whichever way it may be taken, all modern authority points almost without exception to the Arab. Of course I am not referring in any way to heavy draft or carriage horses, although I believe nothing can equal the Arab for light buggy horses in Australia.

General Tweedie says of the Arabs obtained for the Indian Government: 'It is now considered preferable to select in India Arabian, or oftener, it may be feared, Iraki stallions, from the strings of the jambages (horse-dealers), and it is from this source that many of the privately owned Arabs (so called) are purchased.' Which shows the value attributed in India to even an inferior or half-bred Arab, and brings to our minds that few of the Bombay so-called Arabs were at that time pure. And elsewhere he regrets the introduction of so many counterfeit Arabs into India. At all events, that is an authority for the Arab sire.

An article in the *Australasian*, October 6, 1900, says that ' the bone of the Arab horse is admitted to be of very close texture, superior to that of our English thoroughbreds ; that it is this superiority of the bone that renders the Arab horse so valuable for improving a rundown stock.' This can be set off against Mr. Day and his dodo. Before reading the article I had to kill a young stallion, who, unfortunately, got his leg broken between the rails playing with another young stallion on the other side, and my groom noticed the extraordinary hardness of the bone. He had not previously heard or read of this peculiar hardness. I showed the bone to the late veterinary surgeon Dr. Horton, who had attended my horse, and he was much struck with it.

The *Australasian* also says ' that the advantage of a dash of Arab blood was fully recognised by all Australian Bushmen and stock-riders, than whom few men have better opportunities of testing the stamina of the saddle-horse.'

' Bruni,' in the *Australasian*, September 15, 1900, writes that he had conversed with many old horsemen on the subject of horse-breeding, and almost invariably found that they were of opinion that the best way to improve our light horses was to freely use the Arab. In No. 2 of *The Live Stock Handbooks on Light Horses* it is affirmed of Arab horses in the hunting-field that no day appears too long for them, no country too big, and they make light of the proverbial three days a fortnight. On October 26, 1901, Bruni wrote that the change that had taken place during the last two years in the opinion of horsemen as to the best tpye of horse to stand hard usage on scanty and indifferent food had had the effect of again directing attention to the Arab horse as a sire of hardy useful horses; that some years ago there was a pretty lively discussion among horse-breeders as to the value of the Arab horse as a sire, when, unfortunately, the question was viewed from the point of view of a racing man: the hardihood, endurance, and general useful qualities of the Arab grade were ignored. Then he said that, after being neglected for many years, there was evidence that the Arab horse is again coming into favour, and he mentions that at the present sale of American Arabs in New York, bred by Mr. Huntingdon, an average of 1,840 dollars (£358) per head was obtained. Mr. Huntingdon is referred to in Mr. Speed's article in the *Century*, as having fought single-handed for almost a quarter of a century against the prevailing opinion adverse to the value of the Arabian blood. Are our Yankee cousins fools? Would they have given that amount of money if they had not felt confident that they were getting the worth of it?

'Bruni' (September 6, 1902) also said that it was an odd coincidence that since the Arab had been discredited as a sire Australian horses had degenerated. I venture respectfully to suggest that it is more than a coincidence, and that it is not odd. I contend that it is effect following cause. The same cause led to the same effect in breeding thoroughbreds, as Captain Upton has stated. 'Bruni' also points out that some of the foundation stock of the American trotting-horse were 'Arab grades,' and that, though the Arab went out of form in America, as in Australia, there are signs that he is coming in again in the estimation of the American horse-breeders, and he quotes the *Horseman* (Chicago and New York), to the effect that 'the American Arab type was with them to-day.' He adds that in conservative England and in enterprising America there is a decided tendency to use the Arab stallion as a sire, and is evidently surprised that it is not the same in Australia. Mr. Tom Mann, quoted above, shows the reason. Young Australia merely inquires as to what gee-gee he is to back!

The *Town and Country Journal*, September 22, 1900, said that there had been no degeneration in the class of Arabs brought to India during recent years; that the breed had maintained its popularity among Anglo-Indians and natives for all purposes, off the racecourse; and that Arab stallions were much used in the Government studs to improve the country-bred horses. Of course, as the *Town and Country Journal* says, there was no degeneration. It is a pure breed.

The *Register*, March 1, 1901, writes of an interview with Colonel Wyndham, that he said that the style of horse we should breed from was a 'good stallion, well-bred and thick-set, one of the big little class,' which exactly describes the pure Arab.

Mr. M. McRae ('Rainbow') wrote in the *Australian*, March 30, 1901, that the remedy for the improvement of the breed of horses was for the Government to subsidize importers of Arab stallions, or import a few good ones and lease them to the different districts; that if this were done he was sure there would be a great improvement in our horses in a few years, for the Arab has a knack of transmitting his good qualities to his stock. Of course he does, because the Arab is a pure breed of very high antiquity. The thoroughbred, Mr. McRae said, was all very well for racing, but does not come up to the Arab cross for general purposes or to breed for remounts. Of course he does not, because he is not a pure breed.

The *Australasian Pastoralist Review*, November 15, 1900, comparing Arabs and English thoroughbreds, said that it was foolishness to compare the two types when considering the improvement of the

WHAT SORT OF HORSE TO BREED

horse for useful purposes; that the Arab or horse of the Arab type was only worthy of consideration for this purpose; and that those who decry the Arab and laud the English racer, with his straight conformation of hip and shoulder bones, could only do so honestly from a lack of practical knowledge of the subject. I must defend those who laud the English racer from this charge of dishonesty. They honestly do believe what they say, and they are right in saying it. What do they say? In fact, that the English racer is the best creature in the world for a half-mile sprint. No one denies it. But, of course, that makes him so much the worse, and so much the more useless for general purposes.

An article in the *Advertiser*, April 4, 1902, dealing with a conference of horse-breeders, refers to an address to them by Major-General Hutton, in which it was said 'there was a great demand in England for small horses of the cob class. The best of them were purchased as polo ponies, and commanded almost fabulous prices.'

The *Advertiser*, April 2, 1902, quotes Mr. Copeland, who said that if he were going out for a week's pig-sticking in the jungle, where there was not likely to be too much fodder procurable, he would far rather take a couple of Arabs than a couple of Walers, because the former would live and look well on stuff that the Walers would hardly lie down on. Mr. Copeland also said that the Walers in

India were, in common with English thoroughbreds, delicate and in need of constant coddling.

In his book 'War-Horses, Present and Future,' Mr. Sydney Galvayne says: 'The remount horse should not be over 15 hands, *though from* 14 *to* 14½ *is perhaps better* with a big bit of quality.' Such is the Arab.

In an article in the *Daily Telegraph*, February 1, 1902, on horses for South Africa, Mr. John Hill, of Marshbrook House, Church Stretton, mentions his experience with the ponies in his neighbourhood, the largest of which were 12 hands 2 inches, some typical mares averaging only 10 hands, which he put to an Arab sire, and the result was a handsome, compact, and hardy stock averaging 13 hands. He verifies the statement that the race from which the Cape horse started was undoubtedly that of the Barbs and Gulf Arabs imported by the Dutch East India Company at the end of the seventeenth century; and he advises that the new settlers in South Africa should be encouraged to buy ranches, and be given every facility to procure Arab stallions.

An article in the *Spectator*, July 19, 1902, says that 'to breed polo ponies is a matter of careful mating and judicious crossing between our ancient native stock (the wild ponies of the moors) and thoroughbreds or Arab blood.' Showing that to breed from Arabs 'has money in it.'

Of the Arab pony Mr. Sydney Galvayne writes

that it certainly was marvellous how strong they were; many ponies, apparently much stronger, cannot do half what the Arab can. One small Arab stallion carried Mr. Galvayne and his kit sixty miles one day, and did not seem a bit distressed about it; and he says that it is seldom you meet with a vicious Arab, or, indeed, one with any bad tricks at all. Their docility is admirable.

He also writes that an Arab stallion put to Australian and South African ponies will, or should, produce a perfect small army horse or mounted infantry pony, and that the remount horse should not be over 15 hands, with a big bit of quality.

Further on he returns to the subject, and thinks there is only one sort of pony that will do for mounted infantry—viz., the pony with an Arab sire. The Arab is naturally good-tempered, not excitable, yet full of spirit and game. He can do a long day's journey, and repeat the performance for several consecutive days, seemingly with the minimum of fatigue to himself and to his rider. His paces are comfortable, his size, strength, and general appearance suitable. He describes the Basuto pony, which I have already shown, on the authority of Professor Wallace and others, to be descended from Arabs, and which Mr. Galvayne says is a 'really wonderful little fellow. Small, compact, strong, and active, weight never seems to trouble him at all. . . . The writer rode a mite of a thing thirty miles in one day over a frightfully bad country. . . . And the pony not only carried his burden well, but carried it as though it did not trouble him in the least.'

Mr. Galvayne had noticed the weakness of the 'Pall Mall swells' for high horses, which I have above alluded to. He writes that these gentlemen had 'a strong prejudice against the South African horse on their arrival. . . . They saw simply a rather mean-looking pony, with a long tail, instead of a flash-looking English cob with no tail. But the mean-looking pony never came back with a bad report.' As at Omdurman, the 'no-tailed, flash-looking English horse,' beautiful in the Park and admired of damsels, was useless for work, and had to be discarded in both cases for Arab or half-bred Arab ponies.

A writer, 'Merrigang,' speaking of some two Arabs of the Lue Stud of Mr. Vincent Dowling, New South Wales, says that when anybody talks about Arab horses getting small stock again, he will be able to mention these two colts in contradiction; there was a lot of character and massiveness about them; they were wonderfully docile, and make him more infatuated with the Arab than ever.

The *Australasian's* account of Messrs. Campbell and Sons' parade (August 10, 1891) speaks of the attention which breeders had been lately giving to Arabs, and the same paper, in an answer to a correspondent, says that it was a pity the breeding of what they called in Europe 'Anglo-Arab stallions '—

that is, thoroughbred and Arab—was not more practised in Australia.

'Goulburn Valley,' in the *Leader*, October 6, 1890, says that it was contended by some experienced breeders that we want more Arab blood for endurance, and that it was certain that first-class Arab sires of the true breed could only be used at a generally prohibitive fee. On this I observe that it is doubtful if there are any Arab sires in the world of higher class and purer breed than Mr. Blunt's.

The *Mail* (March 9, 1902) states that in a contract by Major Follett for horses for the Transvaal War it was provided that the horse must be within the heights of 14.2 and 15.1 hands. My Quambi Arab stallions have averaged about 14.3 hands; one of them nearly reached 15 hands.

The *Spectator* says (March 15, 1902) that 'nothing can surpass the South African cob for mounted infantry work. They are hardy, active little beasts that require no care, live on the scantiest rations, and on the veldt they are sure-footed as goats. . . . Something is lost even in the Arab if it is bred up over the nominal height of $14\frac{1}{2}$ hands.'

The *Spectator* apparently assumes that the South African ponies are Arabs, as they are. Whether that be his assumption or not, the expression 'even in the Arab' shows the writer's decided opinion of the excellence of the Arab breed, and infers that it would take a great deal to cause that breed to deteriorate. Difficult as that would be, says the writer, 'too greatly increasing its height would cause it to lose something.' I doubt if you could greatly increase its height if you kept the breed pure. If the height were increased by cocktails or hackneys the breed would lose much. Besides, it would no longer be pure Arab.

The *Adelaide Chronicle* (August 23, 1902) writes that a small horse of 15 to 15.2 hands was the type of stallion required for the India markets; a horse 15.3 to 16.1 hands is altogether too large, however well bred.

An article in the *Spectator* (March 15, 1902) says 'that the English riding-horses are condemned as "too long on the leg." To stand campaigning, a beast must be compact and short-legged.'

I think it is Major-General Tweedie who cites a shrewd judge as saying that a good big horse may beat a little one over a short course, but at three or four miles a good little one would beat the biggest he ever saw; and another writer has said that he would go further, and assert that a moderate, medium-sized horse would beat a good big one. But the 'horsey swell' prefers to be high up in the world!

The *Spectator* lays down that it is clear that the same sire which produces a racehorse is not needed to procure a good cross-country riding-horse; nor would the best racing blood ever be available, if only on account of the cost for such a purpose. This gives the key to much of the mischief. The cost of the best blood is prohibitive ; the cost of the worst is cheap : therefore the worst is used.

The Indian Commission recommends breeders to breed horses from 14.2 to 15.2 hands. Mr. Galvayne's book says they should not be over 15 hands, though from 14 to 14.2 hands was better.

'Hackney' (July 28, 1900) writes that both Germany and Russia were buying this 'nuggety' stamp of horse, about 15 hands high, for cavalry purposes.

G. L. Singleton (*Australasian*) maintains that, if the States were to import entires for the improvement of our saddle-horse, they should be of Arab blood, and suggests that without great expense a commencement could be made by purchasing Arab entires for our agricultural colleges.

Mr. Tattersall, in a paper read before the Farmers' Club in England, so long ago as March, 1871, cited by Mr. De Vere Hunt, says that ' the sort of animal wanted to carry troopers was a shortlegged, active hunter . . . not the Leicestershire horse,' and, referring to this paper, Mr. De Vere Hunt affirms the justice of Mr. Tattersall's theory as to degeneracy of our general breed of horses, and sets out a letter from the Master of the Horse to the King of Italy, stating that it was necessary that horses should not exceed 15 hands high.

Mr. Day, while lauding the thoroughbred, now a high, leggy horse, admits that it is singular that such gameness, as well as physical power of endurance, should be so much more frequently evinced by the smaller sort of horses than, comparatively speaking, the larger, yet that it is so, he says, is an indisputable fact. This shows—some of Mr. Day's other utterances notwithstanding—that in breeding the modern English thoroughbred the breeder has neglected the valuable useful qualities for long-leggedness and sprinting. Indeed, so far from being singular, that gameness and power of endurance are more frequently evinced by the smaller than the large horses, it would be singular if it were otherwise, because neither gameness nor endurance, in the true sense, is required for sprinters, and those qualities have been bred out in favour of long legs.

The Vienna correspondent of the *Mail* (February 7, 1902) says that the Hungarian horse has special qualities of endurance, which he attributes to his dash of Arab blood; that it was a great matter to have a certain strain of Arab blood, for the Arab horse and the horse with Arab blood would feed on indifferent forage which the English horse would not look at it, and would retain condition when the latter was reduced to a bag of bones.

Mr. G. M. Curr, in his book,* says 'that all that he saw only led him the more decidedly to endorse the opinions of those who spoke well of the Arab;

---

* 'Pure Saddle-Horses.'

he never met a man who had tried him and did not like him ; he found him in tractability, constitution, durability, soundness, abstemiousness, temper, courage, and instinct, eclipsing and surpassing all other horses that it had been his chance to meet with, and even half-breeds sprung from him were remarkable on this point.

I speak with just something more than book-learning—what I may call a semi-practical knowledge—of the Boer ponies, because my sons have ridden them, and have told me what they can do. They have chased them, and been chased by them, and saw that our horses stood no chance with them. They served as volunteers in the South Australian Fifth Contingent in the Transvaal War, and were nearly fifteen months with Colonel De Lisle, riding about 20,000 miles, in that time fighting or chasing almost day by day, at Grotsvlei, Grasspan (or Reitz), the relief of Benson, etc.; and they affirm that the wonderful endurance of these fine little creatures has in no way been exaggerated. Their Arab origin is unmistakable. The first thing my sons noticed when they made their acquaintance, not then knowing of their Arab origin, was 'how like the Quambi Arabs the heads of these ponies are.' The Transvaal War was not the first time that lack of Arab blood led to mischief in South Africa. Major Tweedie writes (p. 168) 'that if one or two of the splendid Arabs which the late Emperor of the French collected had been reserved for his ill-starred son, the Prince Imperial, the fateful moment of Zululand would not have found him struggling with his charger.'

In 'A Subaltern's Letters to his Wife' (Longmans, Green and Co., 1901), after enumerating eight or ten types of horses used during the Transvaal War, the author says : 'There is not a shadow of doubt that, other things being equal, a small horse is the best in warfare. The country-bred horse of South Africa is the best animal of his inches in the world. He is marvellously hardy, easy in his pace, clever as a cat over holes and bad ground, generally fast, and up to a surprising amount of weight. He is, besides, generally of excellent temper, without vice or tricks, trained to stand for hours in the same place by himself, and wonderfully good-looking, and he adds that there can be no doubt that, for military operations in any part of the world, the Cape or Orange River Colony horses are unsurpassable ; they possess almost every qualification required in a charger.'

Sir Walter Gilbey, without denying the theory that some of the English ponies descended from Spanish horses (themselves Barbs), puts it as more likely that it is to be traced to the introduction into Connemara of the Barb or Arab blood, in about 1833. Whichever it was, it was Eastern. Even after the breed had greatly deteriorated, when the influence of the Barb or Arab blood was dying out, Mr. John Purdon, quoted by Sir Walter, says of some of them, the property of Mr. William Lyons, that they were beautiful mares—he never saw lovelier mares. These ponies 'showed the characteristics, implanted by the infusion of Barb blood, in their blood-like heads and clean limbs.' The reader will again note the sequence, dying out of the Arab blood, and consequent deterioration.

It will have been observed that many of the authorities cited have dwelt upon the necessity for low horses. This was overwhelmingly shown by the Boer War, and has been since admitted and insisted upon by the order of the War-Office authorities, which is, in fact, a policy of return to the Arab. The Arab is, and always has been, a low horse. The light riding-horse of old England, considerably founded upon the Arab, was a low horse. In the reign of Henry VIII. an Act was passed (32 Henry VIII.) to require mares to be at least 13 hands, and the sires 14 hands. That shows how low the English horses were. The three great founders, as they have been called (but they were by no means founders), of the 'blood royal' of English horse-flesh — the Byerly Turk, the Darley Arabian, and the Godolphin Arabian— were only 14 hands; and Sir Walter Gilbey, in the *Live Stock Journal* Almanack, 1902, says that so late as 1700 our racehorses only averaged 14 hands : he cites an author of a book on horses in 1836 who states that excessive height had diminished stoutness, ability to carry weight, and staying power.

Even then the evils of breeding for speed and speed only were being felt. He then cites the late Hon. Francis Lawley, of unrivalled personal knowledge of racing for more than fifty years, who mentions many crack horses of barely 15 hands which had won the Grand National. Mr. Lawley says that few heavy weights who have gone well and straight across country will fail to tell you that they have been better carried by a small horse than a big one. He adds that the great Earl of Jersey, who was at one time invincible for the Two Thousand Guineas, and who won the Derby, used to sneer at a big hunter, who, as he said, could not carry himself, and how could he carry a rider?

That preceded the cabby in *Punch*, who, when told by his fare that he should give his beast some more oats, replied: 'Sure, sir, it's as much as ever he can do to carry what he's got already.' Perhaps the cabby had read of the Earl of Jersey.

Sir Walter continues that height in itself is no advantage whatever, and, being too frequently due to disproportionate length of limb, great height is, speaking generally, a defect; the qualities we should desire in the hunter are usually found in a short-legged, short-backed animal. He then again cites an authority to show that large horses can only be reared on very unnatural food; that they are less stout than small ones under exertion and take more time to recover, and do not carry weight as well.

He then adds his own opinion that it is to be

borne in mind that the above was written at a period when the saddle-horse was in far more general use for road travel than it has been since the spread of railroads, when the saddle-horse was used to make long journeys, and was esteemed in accordance with his ability to carry his rider comfortably and easily at all paces day after day; and he concludes with the remark that space forbids lengthy consideration of the superiority of small horses over large animals under the trying conditions of warfare.

In his book 'Small Horses in Warfare,' published in the year 1900, Sir Walter Gilbey gives numerous examples of the greater endurance and independence of luxury which have been exhibited by small horses in campaigns or travelling in every part of the world. There can be no question whatever but that this superiority has been proved past challenge. This is still more emphasized by the report of the yeomanry in South Africa.

These are the present circumstances of Australia. The horses required to be bred here and for India, except for racing and heavy cart-work, are just the horses spoken of by Sir Walter Gilbey.

The Arab improves every breed he touches, even the Suffolk punch, which, I have read, has Arab blood in him. Of these useful cart-horses Mr. Adye says that they are very docile and willing, and extraordinarily stanch in the collar, a whole team of them having been known to pull at a dead weight till they went on their knees together.

Even in conservative England, notwithstanding jockey-boys, and gamblers, they are beginning to wake up.

A Polo-pony Stud-Book was started in England in 1894. In the preface it is stated that people ride ponies as hacks a great deal more than formerly, while 'at present' there was no distinct breed of riding-ponies.

This proves the growing tendency everywhere in favour of low horses, also illustrated by the new army policy in that direction. But I venture to question the dictum that there is no distinct breed of riding-ponies, because the author says he means ponies of 14 to 14.2 hands, and the latter height may be taken to be the height of the Arab, and the description he gives of the sort of horse required is exactly the description of a somewhat low Arab.

I have looked through the Stud-Books of these polo-ponies for the first three years—-viz., 1894, 1895, 1896—and of its registered stallions I find that in 1894, 25 out of 57; in 1895, 22 out of 30; and in 1896, 11 out of 26—in the three years, 58 out of 113—are Arabs or of immediate Arab descent, and others probably so—more than half for certain! What nonsense, then, to talk of the Arab being as extinct as the dodo for practical purposes! If the pure old English ponies sufficed of themselves, why are more than half the list of Arab blood? Not to forget that nearly all the breeds of English ponies have been improved,

WHAT SORT OF HORSE TO BREED

as above related, by Arabs. So there may be said to be balm in Gilead, after all!

'Bruni' (April 30, 1904), says that at Bolinda Vale a large number of horses are bred, and there are some very attractive youngsters by thoroughbred, trotting, hackney, Arab, and pony sires. The half-bred Arabs are a most promising lot, excellent movers, showing good bone, good shape, good disposition, and having capacity for work.

CHAPTER XI

WHAT OTHER COUNTRIES ARE BREEDING

OTHER countries are setting us an example of what horses we ought to use in order to breed from. The report of the Inspector-General of horse-breeding operations in France for 1899, in his list of stallions serving that year, enumerates amongst others 105 Arabs, 260 Anglo-Arabs, and 164 Southern half-breeds having a strong strain of Arab blood.

Sir Walter Gilbey says that there is only one Government stud-farm, at Pompadour, and that there English thoroughbred Arabs and Anglo-Arab horses only are bred.

Hungary has two studs of half-bred Arab mares, two studs of the ancient blood of Lippieza, which is a mixture of Spanish and Arabian blood, Spanish being largely Arabian. Colonel Horváth gives the numbers: 136 half-blood Arabs, 113 Lippieza (which are themselves half Arab). The stallions used included pure Arabs or half-breeds.

In Austria it is said, 'The Lippizenne horses have marked character of their own, having been obtained

RAFYK (ARAB STALLION).

from Spanish, Italian, and Arab stock; the Spanish itself, of course, strongly tinctured with Arab, the Italian also mixed with Arab. Of course there is considerable Arab blood in the Italian horses from the old Roman foundation stock. In Italy they have 72 English thoroughbreds, 78 Arabs, and 6 Anglo-Arabs.

In Russia, at a Government breeding-stud at Khrénovoi, it is stated 'the best mares here are those got by Arab stallions from English mares.' Streletz 'is devoted to a stud of Arabs, about 20 stallions and 126 mares. At Limarveo, only Arabs are bred.' At Slawuta 'Prince Sanguszko has, or had, a stud of pure Eastern horses, which, Monsieur Salvi observed, shows to what a pitch of perfection the typical Arab can be brought when wisely mated.' Many private owners devote their attention entirely to the Anglo-Arab. This observation as to the pitch of perfection to which the Arab can be brought when wisely mated gives point to Major Upton's argument that it is absurd to say that the Arab is not or would not be as fast as the English horse, even for half a mile, if he were trained for that.

Captain Hayes, in his book 'Among Horses in Russia,' says that the remounts for the Russian cavalry, 'especially those which come from the country of the Don, have a strong infusion of Arab blood, with a dash of the thoroughbred.'

The Ottoman Government possesses four important studs. Since 1892 Arab blood has been introduced. The Arab stud consists of 55 stallions of pure blood and 11 half-bred stallions got by Arabs out of native mares; there are 10 pure Arab mares and 188 half-bred mares. In the second stud, at Sultan Sou, are 12 pure Arab stallions and 7 pure Arab mares. In the Tehoukourova stud are 8 pure Arab stallions and 21 pure Arab mares. The Vezirie stud 'last year (1900) consisted of 10 stallions and 57 mares, all pure Arabs,' and pure-bred stallions —that is, pure-bred *Arab* stallions—are often lent to village communities for the sole purpose of improving the breed of horses.

Sir Walter Gilbey states that in 1886 there were in the Indian stud 146 Arabs.

The *Times* (July 6, 1903), in a report of Mr. Blunt's sale of Arabs on the Saturday before, states that, 'as Mr. Blunt very truly remarked on Saturday, he has had a campaign to fight against the prejudices which any innovation in the matter of horse-flesh meets with from the coachman, the stud-groom, the dealer, and all those whose interests lie in the trafficking of big, corn-consuming, unsound horses.'

It will be observed, as I gladly note, that the *Times* does not mention 'vets.' Then it proceeds to tell us that in all quarters of the globe it is recognised that the Arabian is the best sire for half-bred stock that Mr. Blunt had found that of late years the best customers have been the

Russians, whose purchases have included Mesoaud. Mesoaud is the sire of Faraoun.

The soldiers of all these great military peoples in all quarters of the globe are not fools, surely, when they largely select Arab horses. They must be credited with knowing what they are about. Surely their opinion ought to be of more account on such a subject than that of jockey-boys and bookmakers —even that fine old racing gentleman, Mr. W. Day. The examples just given rather discount his opinion about the extinction of the Arab for practical purposes!

The *Times* also quotes Mr. Blunt's statement, that his plan from the beginning had been to eliminate the idea of great speed as an object to be attained, certainly as a principal object, and he was convinced that the defects of the English thoroughbred were mainly from the sacrifice that had been made of every quality to that of speed. Everybody is convinced of it.

Everywhere the same story: breeding to 'sprint' ruins the breed, and the Arab is the horse to improve and renovate it.

A Japanese buyer in Queensland, January 30, 1904, wants little active horses, 'not the big stamp of animal usually bought by European authorities.' We have very much to learn of the Japanese. A good few people have already learnt something!

An article in the *Century* for September, 1903, by Mr. Charles Gilmer, 'Speed on Horses in

America,' is well worth studying. He pronounced the United States to be the greatest horse-producing country in the world; and he concluded his article with a wail as to thoroughbred degeneracy even in America. He states that the thoroughbreds in America are bred and trained to respond to the demand 'to sprint—that is, to go short distances quickly'—which seemed to him not a good change, except for the gambling game, into which racing has degenerated; for it removes the thoroughbreds of to-day further from the desirable horse type that is needed, and makes them, therefore, much less useful than they might be. Indeed, one can almost believe that Mr. Speed would desire that the remedy should be pursued which he states that Henry VIII. adopted, who issued a sweeping decree that all mares and stallions in the Royal Forests not up to a certain standard should be killed.

What a blessing if that could be done with some of the thousand-pounders!—with all those which are entered in the Stud-Book, and which are therein stated not to be worthy of entry!

It had been supposed that the great Morgan breed of the States was founded upon the English thoroughbred, but Mr. Speed says that he doubts whether, in the making of this type, the thoroughbred blood of England figures at all, and that it is much more likely that it was produced by the union of Arab blood with some other American basic stock. Any other American basic stock must have been more or less founded on the Spanish importations—that is, Andalusians—really Arabs or Barbs, and therefore must have been allied to the thoroughbred blood of England. Mr. Speed did not, apparently, realize how much Arab blood there is in the English thoroughbred. His description of the Morgan type will nearly apply to that of the Arab, and he mentions the Morgan type and the Golddust and Clay types as reproducing types because they were rich in that primitive Eastern blood without which, he says, no great type has ever been created or maintained. Thus, from this thoughtful American is verified the assertion to the effect that the Arab stamps his good qualities on his stock in an unusual degree.

Having shown by every page of his article that this assertion was well founded, Mr. Speed states that the gift by the Sultan of Turkey to General Grant of two stallions — Leopard (Arab) and Linden Tree (Barb)—would probably prove to be a very important event in the history of the horse in the United States. This somewhat differs from Mr. Day's dodo fancy! Mr. Speed proceeds to inform us that among the breeders of horses in America Mr. Randolph Huntingdon has been known for more than forty years, who had always held that blood influence was all-important in breeding, and that kindred blood, when pure, could not be too closely mingled. (Harkaway, with forty-four strains of the Godolphin, for example.) Mr. Speed says that Mr. Huntingdon, being a man acquainted with the history of the horse in the world as well as in America, held that the potent blood in every European type, as well as American type, was of Eastern origin; he therefore hailed the coming of the Grant stallions, and prepared to make use of them by securing some half-dozen virgin Clay mares, themselves rich in Arab blood. With General Grant's consent, Mr. Huntingdon bred these mares to Leopard and Linden Tree, and in a little while had a small collection of the greatest possible interest. He persevered in this for fifteen years, and had developed what he called an American Arab or a Clay Arabian. They were splendid animals—large, shapely, strong, fast, and kindly. Unfortunately, according to Mr. Speed, Mr. Huntingdon had associated with him in the ownership of the horses a New York lawyer—alas, a lawyer!—who proved, in 1893, to be one of the most noted defaulters the United States has known. Mr. Huntingdon was among the victims, and so his valuable and interesting collection had to be sold and dispersed. I do not doubt but that the pure Arab blood would improve the largest animal, as Mr. Speed and Mr. Huntingdon state, but I venture to give a word of warning about breeding horses too large. Modern experience goes to show that it is a mistake to get much beyond 15 hands, and many hold that 14.2 to 14.3 is better for most purposes.

It seems that it was necessary that the American should revert to the Arab, for Captain Pitman, of the 11th Hussars (quoted by Mr. Galvayne in his book), condemns the North American horse as a remount, for the same reason that Mr. Galvayne does. Captain Pitman also believes in the Arab.

Mr. Speed states that Mr. Huntingdon was recognised in England, France, and Russia, as a very enlightened breeder, and among the elect of those who attribute to Eastern blood the rightful virtue. He started again, and his small collection was added to from England by Nazli, a pure-bred Muneghi-Hadruji Arabian mare, with which, and other accessions, he pursued a course similar to that previous to the dispersal of his first collection, until now he has some forty head of horses, pure and half-bred Arabs, and which Mr. Speed states to be the most promising chance that the States have had in some forty years to establish an American type of high character.

The Americans have never been taken to be fools. Indeed, they are recognised as being the most practical people on earth. Is not the policy of Mr. Huntingdon worth considering? Is the opinion of Mr. Speed unworthy of notice? Is a jockey-boy of greater wisdom?

Mr. Speed's article was attacked in the *Century*, January, 1904, by Mr. John L. Hersey, in which is also a reply from Mr. Speed, who cites General Benjamin F. Tracey and Colonel Spencer Borden as supporting his views. The latter gentleman says that the proportion of good trotters of the foals got by the great Hambletonian, about three out of a hundred, does not seem to be very high. Mr. Speed adds that the trotting-horse register was built upon myths, false pedigrees, and forged records, and that not more than two per cent. of standard-bred trotters trot fast, all which, according to Mr. Speed's arguments, shows the necessity of 'creating a proper horse type in America from the basic stock of the country, and the parent stock from which all pure horse types come.' By parent stock he means Arabs.

The following extracts from the report of the Horse and Mule Breeding Commission assembled under the order of the Government of India, 1900-1901, deserve close study, because so much depends on our being able to breed in Australia, so as to suit the Indian market. The report says that the horses allotted to field artillery at Hosur and Ahmednagar were too big; that, as a general standard, a height of 14.2 to 15.1 should be accepted for all horses.

It says that the aim of the Government of India has been to horse all regiments of cavalry, and, if possible, eventually artillery, with country-breds and Arabs only. Note that even the artillery are to have Arabs.

The Commission, previous to visiting the Rajputana and Kathiawar States, had little expectation of seeing any animals worthy of note. They were, however, agreeably surprised to find the opposite the case, and they state that among the Marwari and Kathiawari breeds the general conformation and shape of the head are strongly suggestive of the Arab. This shows that in their opinion the excellence of a breed is in proportion to its approach to the Arab, which further appears by their statement that amongst the young stock of the Rajput stud were several individuals of very high merit got by the direct cross of Arab on Kathiawari mares.

The report also states that the stallions Jim's Coat (thoroughbred) and Hector (Arab) seem to have done excellent work in breeding with the native mares; that there are also two very good stallions by Arab sires out of Kathiawari mares; and so good were they that it raises the question whether in this combination there may not be a possible regeneration of the Kathiawari breed. Observe, again, the Arab brought in to 'regenerate.'

The Commission state that they had been much struck by the loyal endeavours of the native chiefs to breed horses for army remounts by introducing thoroughbred and Arab blood, and that the demand for true Arabs, already great, will probably increase in the future, one of the lessons of the South African War being that small and hardy horses are indispensable, and that there is no breed better calculated than that of the Arab to produce them.

I did not start my stud with the slightest hope or expectation of making a profit—indeed, I fully anticipated a considerable loss—but this statement of the Indian Commission, that the demand for true Arabs is already great, and that it will probably increase in the future, leads me to hope that, even if I do lose, one of my sons may make money out of it hereafter.

The report goes on: 'Out of 124 young stock seen at Ahmednagar, 43 were got by Arab sires . . . they had great quality, and showed true desert Arab type. All the evidence received on the subject clearly proves to the Commission that the small Arab of the desert, which is full of quality and blood, is much better calculated to produce remounts and improve the stock of the country than the big, heavy-shouldered, pig-eyed horses, so-called Arabs, which have been bought during recent years as Imperial stallions. The Commission endorse this opinion from their personal observation.'

Note what emphasis they put on the necessity for the small Arab of the desert, not every big brute who hails from Bombay. Recommendations are then made that the majority of the Imperial stallions should be thoroughbred English or Australian, the rest being Arabs of true desert type, while district board stallions should be Arabs and country-breds; and they say that it is advisable that every district board should have some Arab and some country-bred horses.

Further on they state that at Gujar Khan a number of the young stock were a high class. Sons got by a district board Arab pony Patna were fine big-looking youngsters with plenty of quality. They observe that there was no reason why India should not be allowed to supply her own horses if she could, or at any rate with the assistance of Arabia; and it was very desirable that steps should immediately be taken to provide the supply necessary, so that the whole of the cavalry, British and native, may be mounted on Arabs and country breds. They are hardier than the Australian, and, being smaller, do better on the Government scale of rations. It will be seen by this reference also that the Australian horses have not the good character which they at one time had; the reason is that Australian breeders have neglected the Arab, which they were in the habit of using in the thirties, the forties, and the fifties, and have bred from ill-constitutioned thoroughbred sprinters.

Another illustration—use the Arab, and you get a good breed; drop his use, and your breed deteriorates.

The Commission further point out that the almost unvarying type which seemed to prevail amongst the stock proved that by the intelligent use of highly-bred Arabs and suitable thoroughbred sires, horses of the very best class for Indian remounts could be almost unfailingly produced.

One class of good mares seen at the Sibi fair

was said by experts to be, as a whole, equal to, if not better than, any class of a similar kind to be seen in a show in England, and it was advised that the country-bred mares should have in their pedigree at least two known top crosses of thoroughbred or Arab blood. No distinction is made between English and Australian thoroughbreds. Both are classified as thoroughbred, and a true desert Arab is, of course, undeniably thoroughbred. It will, I think, be difficult, if not impossible, for any fair-minded person, no matter how much prejudiced he may be against the Arab at the outset, to read this report without recognising that in the opinion of the Commissioners the Arab is the horse to rely on—in short, that the Arab is the horse of the future.

It would seem to be a very long way from a lady's new-fashioned frock to the modern breeding of Arab horses, yet the frock brought under my notice a very late reference to that breeding; for on my wife—as wives, I fancy, are wont to do—directing my attention to a pretty gown depicted in her fashion-book, the *Ladies' Field*, October 3, 1903, I noted, on looking at the paper, the pictures of several horses, which I found were pictures from a stud of polo-ponies bred by the Hon. Mrs. Ives, at Moyns Park, Essex, of which there is a long description. The writer says: 'Thoroughbred cross seems almost essential in a modern polo-pony; but any sort of thoroughbred will not do at all—far from it. To carry a heavy man at top speed, to stop and twist and turn in full career without mishap, and to keep this up for ten or fifteen minutes at a stretch, a pony must have plenty of staying power and good obliquely-laid shoulders; and these are not, as a rule, the most conspicuous points in the modern sixteen-hand racing machine.'

Of course not. But they are conspicuous points in the Arab, as I have shown.

The writer adds that there are a few thoroughbred horses to be found which combine the required qualities in perfection, and that it is noteworthy that the majority of those are considerably smaller than the average blood horse, and that amongst those at Moyns Park which have those required qualities was Bashom, an Arab of the highest caste, bred in Arabia by Ibn-Al-Raschid, Sheikh of the northern branch of the Rohilla tribe, thus showing that in using the word 'thoroughbred' Arabs were included.

Then it is stated that among the many wise decisions which led to the final overthrow of the Mahdi's power was the decree that the horses provided to carry our avenging army over the last stages of its march must be desert bred, and that Bashom was one of the many Arabs which joined the British forces for that purpose. On another occasion Bashom had galloped fifty miles in one afternoon with despatches.

In the Park the writer also saw Gossip, the original pony of the stud, a very Arab-looking gray brought out of a Hungarian drove, and Plevna, one of the stud mares, ten years old, bred in the South of France, her sire being one of the Arabs belonging to the French Government stud near Pau.

This description gives additional proof as to the extent to which the Arab is now being generally used, and the passage as to his stopping, turning, and twisting in full career calls attention to what General Tweedie writes of this power, as shown in India, with either a running or charging boar in front of him. So far as regards the polo stud of the Hon. Mrs. Ives, it would seem that all its excellence is really owing to its Arab blood.

CHAPTER XII

CONCLUSION

IN conclusion, I feel it necessary to apologize, to those who may honour me by reading this work, for its shortcomings, which have arisen, first, because the chapters were prepared for Australians only, and were originally prepared for submission to an Australian weekly newspaper as articles on the Arab; and, secondly, because, after they had grown too long for publication in that shape, a severe illness has prevented me from properly recasting them as I would have wished either for shorter articles or for a book. I have only been able to make additions, and at seventy-three, after such an illness, I cannot now face the labour of recasting.

I make no claim to original research or to special knowledge of horses; indeed, I have indulged in no original research at all except looking at two or three articles in the 'Encyclopædia Britannica' (if that could be so deemed) and looking through the military reports. My references to ancient Biblical history are for the most part either from memory of the lessons of a dear and pious mother, who indoctrinated me with the love of such literature when a child, or else from such books as she loved to read to me, most of which I had by me, some of them her gifts, which I have often read wholly independently of, and uninfluenced by, any intention of writing on the subject of the Arab horse—or, indeed, of anything else.

Mr. Day's books and others on the horse which I have referred to I naturally purchased and read when I embarked on my undertaking of endeavouring to introduce the Arab into Australia.

I became the more determined to publish the views I have enunciated, without a thorough revision and without further delay, because 'the night cometh, when no man can work'; because the iron almost of despair, and certainly of indignation, had deeply entered into my soul at our disgraceful repulses in South Africa; and because I realized that those repulses were brought about principally by weedy horse-flesh, and I desired to let my fellow-colonists know—few of them do know—the real excellence of the Arab, whereby I hoped (again I say it) to be able to do some good to my adopted country.

I began by saying that I had no sentiment. Nor had I. But I have now. I think it impossible for any man to call to mind the wonderful deeds that the Arab horse has done, his marvellous faithfulness and obedience to and his caressing affection for his rider, and in return the intense affection for him exhibited by many scores of hard-headed soldiers

CONCLUSION

and business men through all the ages, without feeling sentiment. Job felt it in the beginning of the world, when writing that 'he smelleth the battle afar off.' Major-General Tweedie felt it in these latter days, when he wrote that if we lose him 'we shall never look upon his like again.'

I the more readily submit my views as they stand because no elegance or brilliance of style, even if I had them, would operate on the minds of those who have been educated in, and indoctrinated from their youth up with, the belief of the racing men. Nothing will operate on such minds but repeated and unquestionable authority—repetition as illustrated by the *Times*—even if that do. 'If they hear not Moses and the prophets, neither will they be persuaded, though one rose from the dead.' If they hear not General Tweedie, Field-Marshal Roberts, General Harry Smith, the Ameer Abdul Rahman, the German Emperor, Napoleon Bonaparte, General Daumas, and Abd-el-Kader, with the scores of other experienced men quoted, no rhetoric of mine would amount to much.

APPENDIX I

VARIOUS DESCRIPTIONS OF THE THOROUGHBRED GIVEN IN AUTHORITIES QUOTED IN THIS WORK

Not so stout; not such good stayers; speedy weeds.
Preponderance of unsuitable animals.
Unfit stallions; a lamentable want of good stallions.
Stayers exceedingly scarce.
Useless brutes; ill-bred, nervous, ugly, soft-hearted, and sickly brutes.
No good remounts to be got in Australia.
Never before were there so many complaints of want of constitution, bone, endurance, and ability to carry weight.
General run of horses not nearly so good; strong tendency to deterioration.
Bad fore-legs—quite stilts, in fact.
Spindle-shanked weeds; the veriest weeds.
Horses that would drop before a few miles were covered.
Deplorable deterioration; sadly disappointing.
Rubbish—a disgrace to the men who bred them; never before had such a collection of inferior horses been gathered together.
Not worthy of entry—mere weeds, lacking in the substance necessary.
Strength, stoutness, and courage, for which the breed was once famous, have been completely ignored.
A larger proportion of horses of an entirely unsuitable class.

APPENDIX I

Nervous, fidgety brutes that cannot take part in a parade without being upset.

Shallow in girth and back rib, light in barrel, and from 70 to 80 per cent. of them leggy and deficient in bone and limb.

Diseases of the legs more common among thoroughbred stock—*e.g.*, curb, bone-spavin, bog-spavin, and ringbone.

Not a good horse was to be discovered among them; there was, however, uniformity of bad points.

A pampered stock; not in it for saddle purposes, not having one single recommendation; a most wretched lot.

Bad feet, defective hocks, and other unsoundnesses.

Crooked-legged, deformed brutes, not worth sixpence; useless animals.

Our English troop-horses have altogether collapsed.

A lack of stamina; mediocrity.

The spurious gaining ground every day.

A very bad lot; an unsatisfactory affair; much of a muchness; cut up wretchedly; of poor class.

Most unsound, weedy wretches; roaring increased.

Big hungry chargers; worthless sires; Salvador utterly disgraced himself.

Broken-down crocks and jades nervous and irritable in temper.

Trained only to scramble off from the starting gate on his toes.

Half a dozen horses in one afternoon steeplechasing, with the tube after tracheotomy in their throats.

Unsound, weedy half-milers or four-furlong shadows.

APPENDIX II

I HAVE thought it excusable to give a short summary of the opinions of the purchasers of some of my pure-bred young Arab stallions; all these purchasers are, I believe, owners of runs in the interior of Australia in a large way. In no instance have I received one single word of disparagement, and many of the encomiums which I have received have been volunteered.

S. P. Mackay, Esq., of Brunswick, Melville Park, North-Western Australia, who purchased two, Saladin and Jedaan, in 1898, writes:

'They are sleek as hounds, never had a toothful except the natural herbage. I hear great accounts of Saladin's stock. Jedaan has grown a fine animal; his stock are very promising, and handsome as paint, and am sorry I have not more of them.' Again, August 22, 1902: 'I hear great accounts of Saladin's stock. Jedaan is here under my eye, and is everything I could wish; his stock are good and showy as well. . . . I am sure his stock will come out on top. I never made a purchase that has given me more satisfaction.' Again, September 15, 1903: 'Jedaan is very much to the fore at present this winter. His progeny do their work splendidly. Notwithstanding that most of the Bush roads are sandy, they are absolutely stanch, and have no vice. They carry themselves so well that it pays to put nice harness on them.'

F. S. Thompson, Esq., Warrawagine, Condon, North-Western Australia, who purchased Kazim, writes:

'Kazim continues to give us satisfaction; as quiet as ever, and absolutely no vice. His young stock are doing well, and are satisfactory, those out of thoroughbred mares being especially good.'

E. P. Quinn, Esq., of Tarella, Wilcannia, New South Wales, who purchased Assad, writes:

'Assad is growing into a fine horse; a nice shape, with really good legs, and bone like steel. His temper is all that could be desired. A more docile animal was never foaled, and yet he is full of fire and spirit.' Mr. Quinn afterwards purchased Adban, and subsequently, in inquiring what others were for sale, January 1, 1904, writes: 'I am very pleased with the few Assads that I have. They are nearly three years old now, and are all that could be desired. They are handsome and very sturdy. Assad has stamped his stock very much after himself. Adban's stock are faultless as foals. I have nineteen head of as handsome foals by him as I would ever wish to see.' He has since bought a third (without seeing him), a youngster.

Mr. Creed, of Cecilwood, Rockhampton, July 4, 1903, of Barak (then just arrived at Rockhampton), writes:

'I think him a very handsome colt, and should make a very perfect horse. Everyone that has seen him thinks him a fine colt. . . . I am sure there will be no such horse in looks, style, etc., about here. I am very pleased with him.'

Mr. T. H. Pearce, of the *Katherine*, wiring the safe arrival of Ibrahim and Joktan at the station, June, 1904, says:

'They give every satisfaction, and I am delighted with them.'

J. W. Brougham, Esq., of Poolamacca Station, Broken Hill, New South Wales, who purchased Abdallah:

'Abdallah's stock promise well. They are beautifully topped with a fine carriage. His disposition is wonderfully quiet, and a child could ride him with safety.' On a later date he writes: ' He is such a pet; ever so docile.' Again, February 25, 1904, writing to thank me for a newspaper which I sent him, he adds: 'It was rather strange—the day the newspaper arrived my boy brought in from the back-station two of Abdallah's colts, just broken in. He was so proud of them he rode them in to show me, and really they show quality, breeding, and usefulness; perfect hacks, plenty of substance, standing 15½ hands, and only three years (off). Am breaking them in now, and when quiet will let them run till five years; then they will be fit for any work. I would like you to see the youngsters, and you would be still prouder of Rafyk.'

Mr. Warburton, a horse-breeder in Northern Australia, who purchased Zubeir, writes:

' Will you allow me to congratulate you on being the owner of such a horse as Rafyk? I can only say that words fail me to express my admiration for him. I could have spent hours looking at him. There is not such another horse in Australia; he is perfect in every way.' Again, in May, 1904: ' Zubeir is growing very like Rafyk, and is in good trim. He has not had an ounce of stable feed since he has been up here. He is doing good work, and it would take a big cheque to buy him now.'

Mr. C. R. Bunbury, of Williambury, Western Australia, who purchased Khaled:

' I like Khaled very well indeed. He is full of life and quality, and his foals are very handsome. He is very docile when handled, and a good doer.' Again, on September 12, 1903: 'I have broken in a dozen of Khaled's stock lately. They are the quietest and most tractable youngsters I ever had anything to do with, and stand their work well for youngsters.'

Mr. Bush, of Clifton Downes, Gascoyne, Western Australia, July 6, 1903, writes:

' Suleiman is doing very well, and I like his stock very much. Although he is small, his stock are of good size, and if they turn out as well as they look they will be very good. . . . There is no doubt at all they will turn out well. Suleiman is a beautiful-tempered horse.'

Again, on a later date:

'Having only used him for about one year, I am unable, of course, to say anything about his stock. . . . I think he will mate well with the class of mares I have put to him. He is a beautiful-tempered horse, and a good doer, having had to cut his own grass ever since I have had him.'

Of many of the half-breeds sired by my stallion I have had similarly satisfactory accounts.

Mr. A. H. Morris, cattle-dealer and stock-agent, Western Australia, writes, February 5, 1904, to Mr. J. Carwardine, cattle-dealer and stock-agent, by whom he was asked to inspect :

'I went and had a look at the Arabs. Rafyk is a powerful horse, and I like him very much. They have another pure-bred Arab (imported), Faroun. He is a shade finer in the bone than Rafyk, shows more quality about the head ; in fact, all over he is a beautifully-made horse, and worth a day's journey to look at. If you get a chance, go out and see him ; he is a beauty. The pure-bred Arab mares are a nice lot, but Rose of Jericho is quality all over. There are two nice yearling colts (pure Arabs), but both are sold. Mr. Boucaut said three geldings out of Stud-Book mares were at his brother's place, so on my way back I went and saw them, and saw one that I wish had been kept for a stallion. He would have suited me ; he is out of a thoroughbred mare, but has the stout body of the Arab, and has size. He was running loose in the paddock, but I should take him to be about 15.2. You may see him some day ; he is a powerful horse ; he has inclined to the Arab in thickness of wither and neck, but I like him very much. In seeing him I have seen what the cross between the thoroughbred mare and Arab will produce, and I feel satisfied that it is a splendid cross. The other gelding, a chestnut bred the same way, is a totally different horse. He is lengthy, lean, and wiry. I never saw him out of a walk, but if he is not a hard, wiry horse, and a fast one, I am much mistaken. Well, I thoroughly enjoyed myself to-day. How I wish to have money, not for the money's sake, but for what I feel confident I could do in the shape of producing horses that would not only be useful, but horses that would give only one who knew what a good horse was pleasure to look at.'

Neither Mr. Morris nor Mr. Carwardine was known to me!

POSTSCRIPT

AFTER every line of this book and of the Appendixes were written, I applied to a friend, who has a very complete cable code, to be allowed to use it in cabling to London in respect of publishing, and he called my attention to a little book, 'An Appeal for the Horse,' published in Adelaide in 1866 by Mr. George Hamilton, formerly Inspector of Mounted Police of this State, and afterwards Commissioner of Police, who was well known as a remarkably clever judge of horses, concerning which he was a high authority, and he more than justifies my criticisms on grooms and jockey-boys. He says that the majority of the stable fraternity are thoroughly versed in ' an extensive range of ignorance; as wedded to the most dangerous notions as they are to the wives of their bosoms —some of them more so,' and adds that the Arabs might enlighten us on many points, and we might learn a lesson or two from those 'who never put on top-boots in their lives,' evidently having the 'Piccadilly masher' in his eye. Or perhaps the ten-dollar amateur of the *Times*! He speaks of the affection of the Arab for his horse, of which he was a great admirer, and quotes one as saying:

APPENDIX II

'Uncover his back and satisfy thy gaze! Say not he is my horse, say he is my son; he is pure as gold; he has no brother in the world; he is a swallow.'

Mr. Hamilton, whose opinion about horses no one would have gainsaid in his lifetime, then relates some interesting anecdotes in favour of the Arab horse, which he himself learned from an Arab tribe in Egypt. The high reputation which he enjoyed has induced me to add this postscript.

THE END

www.ingramcontent.com/pod-product-compliance
Lightning Source LLC
Chambersburg PA
CBHW032106220426
43664CB00008B/1155